To Richard
Hope you enjo[...]

# NOWT LIKE THIS IN
# AMERICA

## AN UNTOLD HISTORY OF
## THE 1980 STEEL STRIKE

**Theatre is real life**
grown up dramas for the young at heart

Published in paperback in 2023 by Sixth Element Publishing
on behalf of Alan Spence

Sixth Element Publishing
Arthur Robinson House
13-14 The Green
Billingham TS23 1EU
www.6epublishing.net

© Alan Spence 2023 ,

ISBN 978-1-914170-46-1

British Library Cataloguing in Publication Data. A catalogue record for this book is
available from the British Library.

Printed in Great Britain.

# NOWT LIKE THIS IN AMERICA

## AN UNTOLD HISTORY OF THE 1980 STEEL STRIKE

The story of a family,
a community and an industry

## ALAN SPENCE

Theatre is real life
grown up dramas for the young at heart

*"Television is wallpaper,*
*Cinema is dreams,*
*but Theatre is real life."*

Matthew Kelly

# ACKNOWLEDGEMENTS

Thank you to Nigel Kellaway who has supported me, not just on this project, but for so many creative things, and I am forever grateful. http://nigelkellaway.co.uk/

A big thank you to the cast, for giving up their time and sharing their creativity with us all and for putting up with my little jokes. To my sister Judith and her husband Peter who went above and beyond to enable me to finally realise a full production.

To Gillie and Graeme at Sixth Element, who continue to be a sublime mixture of creativity and to have a common-sense business approach.

To Tony (Jack) McBride who dazzled us all, in the early days of Grangetown Boys' Club and no matter where he travelled or worked, he always wanted to lend a helping hand.

To John Benton (Michael Gunn) a local lad who certainly made something of himself in the business, and my best friend, always encouraging others and of this play, he said, "I love that you have written it in the local vernacular." I do so miss him.

To my sister Janice and friends who always supported me and told me to keep on writing, Dawn for offering to proofread the book and Laura… they put up with my dreams and they still love me.

# CONTENTS

# PART 1: BACKGROUND

## About The Author

Alan Spence was born and brought up in South Bank, Middlesbrough. After failing the 11+, he took on a range of 'industrial guises' including shipyard welder, maintenance man at South Bank Coke Ovens, student nurse, and tele-sales advertising. He even tried working in a men's clothes shop, for a whole morning.

After living in London, a return to Teesside saw Alan back at British Steel Corporation on the Redcar Coke Ovens, and faced with what he has always seen as two strokes of luck: firstly, the 1980 Steel Strike (the subject of Alan's first play) and secondly, redundancy, which enabled Alan to go to Middlesex Polytechnic and train for a BEd in Drama and History, for which he achieved a 2:2.

Alan spent twenty-five years as an arts practitioner in secondary schools, gained an M.A. in Film and Television from London University and he even ran his own theatre company, Theatre is Real Life, from 2009 until 2018.

He is member of the Writers' Guild of Great Britain and serves on their Theatre Committee, and is also a member of National Drama and sits on the steering group of the Drama and Theatre Education Alliance. Alan is a Drama and Theatre tutor at the Printers Playhouse, Eastbourne.

This is Alan's second published play, following The BORO's 37mins published 2022. His other plays include: My Name is Tom (2016) Homes and Gardens (2018) and Abandoned (2022).

"*The Theatre of Action realises that the very class which plays the chief part in contemporary history — the class upon which the prevention of war and the defeat of reaction solely depends — is debarred from expression in the present day theatre.*"

Joan Littlewood

# "Don't put your kids on the stage... Mrs Worthington."

Teesside has always played its part in the entertainment of the nation with musicians such as Paul Rodgers, David Coverdale, Chris Rea and James Arthur.

Then there is South Bank's Florence Easton who made it all the way to the Metropolitan Opera in New York, opera singer Suzannah Clarke, pianist Richard McMahon, cellist Caroline Dale, and the Apollo Male Voice Choir.

Actors and comedians include Wendy Richards, Thelma Barlow, Bob Mortimer, Wendy Craig, Roy Chubby Brown, Richard Griffiths, Jamie Bell, Monica Dolan, Mark Benton and Elizabeth Carling.

Writers of all genres include Pat Barker, Ishy Din, Reg Smythe, Adele Parks, Harry Pearson, Richard Milward, Graham Farrow, Ann Jellicoe and E.W. Hornung of the famous Raffles crime stories. Film and television is no less sparkly with Franc Roddam, Steph McGovern, Kirsty O'Brien, Jeff Stelling and Chris Kamara.

Of course, some of those success stories weren't even born before I started treading the boards, by engaging in performances. This is just as well really because I was an unmitigated disaster. I kid you not. To be fair, my Mam and Dad had no pretentions for me at all, but I had to go to school every day, work hard, leave school and get a job, preferably a trade. Unlike me Dad, but therein lies another story.

Butter wouldn't melt

I suffered from chicken pox and scarlet fever as a four-year-old. Memories of that fever can easily be evoked and the downstairs front-room darkness looms large in my mind's eye. Why was I so hot? Why was I on my own? Didn't anyone care about me?

Of course, you get through these things, of course you do. Even if you don't know how or why, after feeling so dreadful. Perhaps someone was looking after me, and had me mapped out for greater things? But before I could say, "Mam, can I go out to play now?" I found myself back in hospital, North Riding Infirmary, in Newport Road, this time with suspected Tonsilitis. My one abiding memory, apart from feeling horrible again, was of a towering, red-headed and freckled SEN, wearing a green gingham uniform.

That nurse was the culprit, who almost sat on me because I dared to try and fight when I was being put to sleep. They were using what looked like a 50's radio mike and a gas called Halothane. But the good news was at least this newly introduced gas was no longer inflammable. Great! That hospital is now an Aldi supermarket. Karma?

This was my early development, in a South Bank community with a population of just over 11,000 according to the 1951 census. We were surrounded by shipyards, railways and dwarfed by the steelworks, growing up in a family of six, regular periods of sickness, with a Dad on shifts, in a two-up two–down, post-war terraced house. Despite all this, these were happy times, with magic memories.

My first school was Upper Princess Street School just two blocks away, straight up the road, albeit over the busy Nelson Street and even busier Middlesbrough Road, but within walking distance. My brother Peter attended the Juniors, and I, the Infants.

I can't remember how I got involved in The Green Imp. Was I chosen? Had I volunteered even? Did they see me as a show off, or an infant prodigy perhaps? I have no recollection.

This innocent school performance required me to sing, dance or rather move around and wear a green crepe paper costume and with green powder paint on my face. This was 1952/53, and a long way before David Bowie! That outfit? They were obviously taking no chances, as to everyone knowing who or what I was, and certainly not relying on my acting and performance abilities.

I can't remember any rehearsals or should that be practices? When the day of the performance came, I suffered from stage-fright, not that I knew what that was. I was so nervous, I vomited into the sink as I was getting washed for school. This had never happened before; I was even more scared. Surely, I was too ill to perform? How could I go to school now?

With no further sickness that morning, Dad decided I could go to school after lunch, trust him to be on night shift. You can't let them down. Your audience needs you. What, to totally humiliate myself? Suffice to say, like a rabbit in the headlights, I went through the motions of…

Here comes the Green Imp, the Green Imp, the Green Imp
Here comes the Green Imp, the Green Imp, the Green Imp
To scare you all away.

If anyone heard anything I said or sang beyond the first row of seats, it would have been a miracle. No plaudits, not a sausage. I was very ill that morning and I'd made a real effort to be there. Message to self… never again. I'm sure the teachers were saying the exact same thing.

South Bank was blessed with not one, but three cinemas. The Empire was the only purpose built theatre and opened before WWI, The Hippodrome was a corrugated sheet of a monstrosity that screened magic and music, and The Majestic was a functional 60's brick building, that served as cinema, public house, and even as a nightclub.

The Majestic was where my sister had her wedding reception. All three served to fuel my interest in film and music from Rock Around the Clock to Annie Get Your Gun and Mario Lanza in The Student Prince.

It was at the cinema in the mid-1950s that my brother and I were introduced to Dean Martin and Jerry Lewis, a nightclub comedy duo who made it big in Hollywood.

It was my second venture into performing. Well, this was enacting a scene from the film we had just watched at the cinema, perhaps 3 Ring Circus or You're Never Too Young. My brother Peter was the smooth and sensible Dean Martin and no prizes for

50's comedy gold
Dean Martin and Jerry Lewis

guessing I was the zany and eccentric Jerry Lewis. With no script, we just tried to improvise from memory, well I did anyway. Sometimes it worked, or were Mam and Dad just putting up with me? But I sensed a difference to what had happened when I nervously did The Green Imp. I wanted to be Jerry Lewis, I wanted to perform, I felt… empowered. Was I turning into a show-off?

With the birth of my younger sister Janice, we moved to the new council estate that still had the steelworks as a backdrop on one side. It also had a vast expanse of land where the slag deposits were left, hence my hometown forever became affectionately known as Slaggy Island. What a playground to get you out of the house, and from under everyone's feet. What a space to play hide and seek, a moon-landing of a place, long before 'the smallest step for a man, and the biggest step for mankind'. It was Buster Crabbe meets Doctor Who, but you had to be careful, one wrong step and you could do yourself serious damage. No health and safety in those days.

The other side of the estate was Dales Farm and acres of fields, which I had to cross to go to my new school, Beech Grove Juniors. There were often cows in the fields, so you had to keep an eye on them and dodge many a cow pat, not easy on mornings when you were half asleep. Mind you, my journey to secondary school was to go left at the fields. Fields that were ploughed on a regular basis and not only slowed you down, but also you arrived at school with the filthiest shoes ever. Was it worth the aggro and embarrassment? But if you missed the one school bus, which often came early, you had no choice!

The approach to Beech Grove Juniors was down a long tree-lined street of large 1930's houses, a far cry from the terraced environs

of Upper Princess Street School. The new school had classrooms that were bigger, often dual aspect and looked out onto green spaces, beyond which was our own football pitch.

In 2017, I got the chance,

My old school classroom in 2017

along with other old South Bankers, to take part in a very special event at the newly refurbished South Bank Primary School. We talked about our lives after leaving South Bank, and the group included business people, military personnel, Olympic athletes and swimmers, a former policeman and now Blues DJ, and myself, the teacher. It was a great experience, talking to Year 2 up to Years 5 and 6 and I wouldn't have missed it for the world. I felt very special, as we all did, wanting to give something back.

One unexpected pleasure was to visit the old Beech Grove school site next door, which now provides a range of education support services. So glad they didn't knock it down!

Beech Grove Juniors gave me three lasting memories: another performance disaster, my first crush and an invitation to audition for the local church choir.

Having failed miserably as the lead in The Green Imp at South Bank Juniors, I was given a supporting role in the 1957 Beech Grove School Production of The Nativity, I was a king no less, Melchior, the one who brought the gold! Hardly a demotion.

On the performance day, in a packed hall, I remember us as the three royal Magi making our way, treading carefully and as royally as we could, on to the blocks that acted as the stage in those days, to join Mary, Joseph and the baby doll Jesus, wrapped in a tea towel, carrying our precious gifts in solemnity, for our new born King.

Before I could say those immortal words, "Sire, I bring you gold," I blacked out into a crumpled heap. Silence. The next thing I remember was waking up in a teacher's arms and being carried to the medical room. Well? Just what happened there? I was given a cup of tea and a biscuit and with no further symptoms of anything, I was sent back to my classroom. Perhaps I was sickening for something? Such confusing emotions, crushes, don't you think? I couldn't say why this all happened, but perhaps it was part of growing up. Miss Burns, yes, she was nice. She could also shout, you mark my words. So, what was it? Spending time on a daily basis with another women, other than my Mam?

She looked a bit like that, with her weeny horn-rimmed glasses.

Sometimes, I just used to stare at her from a distance rather than getting on with my work, wishing she would come and help. When she did come to our table, I pretended I knew what I was doing, head down and my arm covering my book, as if I was working, working really hard. Obviously not hard enough, as I went on to fail the 11+ plus, unlike my brother Peter and younger sister Janice.

But one memory that still stands out at Beech Grove, is that someone, I never knew who, was it Miss Burns, had secretly

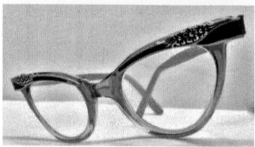

been keeping an eye on me. They recommended that I audition to join the St John's Church choir. Me sing in a church? With the choir? Now where the bloody hell did that come from? I don't sing, I sort of yodel, like Frank Ifield. My asthma remained undiagnosed for a further thirty-odd years. And did I tell you, I couldn't read music? What sort of choir would take someone like me? Another disaster, just waiting to happen?

While I was totally unprepared for my choir audition, Choirmaster Bill Readman, a music teacher from the local grammar school, was very pleasant and welcoming. Standing next to the church organ, in the half light of an evensong, I had no idea what I was doing and what he thought of my utterances. Bill's approach was both nerve-wracking and yet nice, as he leaned over, trying to catch anything he thought I was projecting. Did I have a voice? Was I in tune? Did I have an ear? I couldn't hear myself copying the notes he played. Thank goodness he didn't ask me to sight-read… that embarrassment would come later.

St John's Choir was a real commitment, with choir practices on Mondays and Wednesdays, and two services on a Sunday: Holy Eucharist and Evensong. While most of my friends were footballing on the green, going off to Conker Wood, playing on their bikes and/or skates, I was stuck in church. Why did I feel I was the one with the misspent youth?

St John's Church, South Bank

There were also weddings and christenings on Saturdays and Sundays, especially in the summertime and worth 2s 6d, the equivalent… £3.55 today.

That said, it was a hard slog and I was playing catch up from day one. I couldn't read music, remember, so rehearsing the psalms, which were rehearsed and sung using numbers 1 to 10 or 1 to 20, while trying to hold on to the tune was a challenge. How did I manage? Very badly. Doing everything by guesswork and/or memory at best, while yodelling (because of my asthma) like Frank Ifield singing 'I Remember You'. Why did I put up with it? Did I like the music? Yes, I did. Did I think I could sing? No. Then there was a fateful wedding day. We never knew who was getting married. Their banns were read out at church on Sundays, but none of it registered. It was just another half-a-crown.

Not this Saturday. This particular wedding was different. Why? Wasn't it just another short and stout dark blue pin-striped guy, balding hair slicked-back, trying to look smart. Looking up the aisle for his bride, nervous, desperate or both? He looked old before his time. Imagine my horror to see the lady who had kept him and all of us waiting, the lovely Miss Burns. Miss Burns, how could you do this? To make matters worse, I was on her side of the church, so she had to walk past me to go into the vestry and sign the register, a final act of betrayal. Did Miss Burns live happily ever after? Who cares.

After that, why bother? Well, there was the music. A choir on form is a glorious sound. Moments of belonging, a thoughtful and caring sermon, all helped to play their part. But then churches were a potent form of theatre when the masses could neither read nor write, dazzling us into heaven or damning us into hell. Perhaps not quite as dramatic as that but being in the choir helped nurture my interest in stories and narratives, in the staging of those narratives and what they could convey.

Being a choir member, there were plenty of other happenings and one-off events, such as the Festival of Remembrance at Middlesbrough Town Hall, choir camp to Leyburn in the Dales, which were some of the sunniest places of my teenage years and the Diocesan Festival of Choirs at York Minster. Singing carols at Normanby Hospital or Poole Sanatorium, for those unfortunate enough to be in hospital at Christmas, all contributed to my growing love of all types of music, of performance and a sense of service, of being part of something different.

We used to get amazing spreads, especially at Normanby, where there would be a table full of sandwiches, sausage rolls and iced minced pies, as far as the eye could see. What joy! The Festival of the Nine Lessons and Carols with the choir entering the church and a solo treble voice leading us into Once in Royal David City was so powerful. Is that why music is such an integral part of my playwriting and productions?

Also at Christmas, parishioners could have a visit from the choir for a small donation to the Church Funds of course. The outreach didn't stop there. The Senior Citizens' Club met on a Wednesday afternoon and a cup of tea with biscuits was the usual fayre, an occasional speaker, a beetle drive or a game of whist.

Once again, I found myself, along with my fellow choristers, in a performance I knew nothing about or how we got involved. We had to sing the classics from the Black and White Minstrel Songbook: Lily of Laguna, My Old Kentucky Home, Me and My Shadow, to name a few. That's enough, if you are of a certain age, but they will be in your head for ever more. We thought we were being helpful, but it came at a cost as we young and innocent entertainers had to wear the black face makeup associated with the Minstrels. Did it really enhance the performance? I doubt it.

There were consequences too. I had a paper round straight after the performance and only had time for a quick wash in the church hall facilities. My paper round took me to houses on either side of the main town thoroughfare of Middlesbrough Road, where each house was some distance from the next, street after street, and up to the far end of the town. It was only when I got back home that I realised all the funny looks, and the double takes, were because I had failed to clean the black stage makeup off my face.

Thankfully there was no racism but this was the early 1960s and anything could have happened. Perhaps someone was looking after me. If only I knew about removing stage makeup! Another lesson for me to learn. However, after a week's holiday in Belgium on the coast at Blankenberg, when I got myself a bit of a tan, I was subjected to racial abuse. You couldn't make it up.

Here's us on Blankenberg beach doing our bit for Page 3, with apprentice mates Stan on the left and Peter on the right, with me in the middle and Trevor on the sand, being Trevor. The shadow, bottom right is Tony, who kindly took the picture.

On my return, I was on a 'N' Corporation bus, going to see my then girlfriend and I was sitting upstairs on an almost empty bus. Someone got up behind me and on their way downstairs, shouted 'P***'. It was a few seconds later that I realised they were abusing me. Why? Because I'd been to Belgium for a week?

Even at secondary school, whatever the artform, danger was still just around the corner. How about Shadow Puppets? The culprit this time was Mr Slater, PE and Science Teacher, very old school, who wore those rugby shorts that had button fastened trousers. Slater had the hots for twin teachers, the Wilson sisters. Everyone could see it.

So, what could possibly go wrong with shadow puppets? It was the tale of a hospital operation, lots of woodwork implements, things being removed for the patient and of course plenty of sound effects: bangs, saws and the inevitable blood curdling screams. One scream you won't have heard, was when Mr Slater, the very same experienced teacher, added one more bit of business to our performance.

All I had to do was hold a rope as if it was some sort of intestine and all Mr Slater had to do was cut it. What did he do? He got too close with the biggest and rustiest of garden shears, cutting not the rope, but the inside of my left bicep and stayed there, drawing blood. My blood. Bearing in mind my nativity experience, if I had been any sort of an actor I could have collapsed in a screaming heap and brought the house down. Instead, I took one for the team and let Slater off the hook. On reflection, I did put in something of a performance, so perhaps I was learning after all?

The final piece of this formative jigsaw belongs to Grangetown Boys' Club. I have already spoken elsewhere of my gratitude to them in my development as a person and who I grew up to be. But in terms of drama and theatre, it was down to Bertram Wood Woolley MBE. Ex-Merchant Navy, then English Teacher and Lecturer, he worked with so many groups which included The Progressives, Middlesbrough Youth Theatre and of course Grangetown Boys' Club.

Bert Woolley relaxing with his paper and pipe

Bert was known throughout the North East and was a contemporary of Michael Croft of the National Youth Theatre, Peter Terson (Zigger Zagger, The Apprentices) and the legendary Dorothy Heathcote.

He was awarded an MBE in 1972 for his services to Drama and Education, which came as no surprise to anyone who knew him. As early as the 1950s, Bert was a regular winner of the National Association Of Boys Clubs Drama Finals.

I joined Bert's drama group in 1966, and was straight in at the deep end with Brendan Behan, Shakespeare, Harold Pinter and Eugene Ionescu. He made no concessions. He nurtured us all along the way while expecting us working class lads to keep up. We loved it.

The drama courses at East Barnby Outdoor Centre were organised by the North Riding Education Committee. I couldn't get enough of them, learning three different play extracts which were performed to an audience at a nearby venue. Other courses included improvisation, movement, poetry and folk songs. This was the 1960s in the middle of the Vietnam War so our anti-war revue where Wilfred Owen rubbed shoulders with Buffy St Marie, gave you a sense that you were being listened to.

Bert was comfortable talking and arguing with any of the lads who took him on. But not in the parental 'children should be seen and not heard' kind of way. He was genuinely interested in what young people had to say.

I remember putting an idea for a play to Bert and he quickly rattled off a series of scenes for me to write. "Is that the first half?" I enquired. "That's the whole bloody play, y'Tyke!" scoffing at my suggestion. Tyke was Bert's

Looking for inspiration or trying to remember my lines?

favourite put down. I knew Yorkshire CC to be known as The Tykes, and it was only later that I discovered that being called a 'tyke' meant being 'a crude uncouth ill-bred person lacking culture or refinement'. Bert always said it with such aplomb, you thought you were being praised!

I performed in two plays with Bert at the Middlesbrough Theatre. The first was The Pied Piper of Hamelin with music by Gwyn Morris and a cast that included a young Coronation Street actor Billy Fellows, Carole Copeland who is a very successful actor and director with Pomegranate Youth Theatre in Chesterfield, and Leslie Salmon. Leslie played the disabled boy who didn't get away and I was her father. Leslie was both a gymnast and a dancer. No one would have guessed… she was so convincing. A very emotional scene.

The Mayor and his Corporation in The Pied Piper

*(Johnny Benton became known as Michael Gunn when he joined the acting profession, Tony Leneghan another GBC member and myself, doing what I was good at, gesticulating.)*

16

The second was Peter Terson's Zigger Zagger, which was the first production by the new National Youth Theatre in 1967 and set in Stoke on Trent. Bert set the play in Middlesbrough, with scaffolding on the stage to create the terraces and over a hundred actors chanting the Boro songs.

It was a fantastic experience.

In the early 1960s, drama was struggling to get a foothold on the school curriculum, and theatre did not emerge as a subject in its own right based on a definition of studying theatre. Yet here was Bert, Grangetown Boys' Club and the North Riding Education Committee, giving both opportunity and commitment for young people to play drama games, engage in improvisation, movement and scripted work, with performances to an audience. Were they ahead of their time? On reflection, I believe they were, and certainly with the cannon of plays Bert introduced us to.

In 1982, I went to college, never thinking in my wildest dreams I would end up working as a Drama Teacher, a GCSE and A Level examiner, running my own theatre company or becoming a published writer.

**Theatre is real life**
grown up dramas for the young at heart

# CAST – 2009 PRODUCTION

## Saltburn Community Theatre, Saltburn-by-the Sea.

*Characters in order of appearance*

**Susan Wilkinson** KELLY HEWITSON

**Maureen Wilkinson** SUE BREWSTER

**Billy Wilkinson** LUKE PITT / KILLIAN CRADDOCK

**John Wilkinson** STUART ADAMS

**Tony Simpson** EDWARD WILKINS

**Mick Evans** CHRIS CUTHBERTSON

**Jeff Starforth** HOWARD FIRTH

**Dick Graham** KEN CAVAN

**Sheila Wallace** KAREN MOORE

**Wendy Martin** LIZA CANDARA

**Brian Wallace** HARRY E. SIMPSON

**Peter Martin** JAMES COPESTAKE

# CREATIVE TEAM

**Director** ALAN SPENCE

**Stage Manager** DAVE HUDSON

**Costume / Props** JUDITH MONROE.

**Crew** JUDITH MONROE, PETER BRUN AND THE COMPANY

**Lighting** SALTBURN 53 COMPANY

**Sound** SALTBURN 53 COMPANY

**Front of House** SALTBURN 53 COMPANY

# A big thank you to so many...

Robert Battersby, Creative Director at Richmond Arts, for projector/screen.

John Bolton and Teesside Cast Products for the equipment and support.

Phil Brown for his photograph of the Redcar Blast Furnace
used in the poster.

Chris Hole at Middlesbrough Evening Gazette for all the coverage.

Peter Jeffers and MC Construction for the lockers.

Lisa McCormack and John Foster at BBC Tees for all the support
and publicity.

Michael Morrisey at Darlington and Stockton Times for your help
and encouragement.

Newboulds, Guisborough, for the sausages.

Vicki Patrick and the 53 Wardrobe Team.

Jeanne Round and Anne Tighe Redcar Community College
for the support and much more.

John Simmons and Saltburn Salerooms for the loan of the furniture.

Darren Smailes for the photographs.

Jeffrey E Smith Butchers for the mince.

Eileen Thomas, School Improvement Officer, Redcar,
for the guidance and media promotion.

Philip Thompson and the SCAA volunteers.

## A VERY BIG THANK YOU...

Jack McBride for believing in the play and communicating it to so many.

My sister Judith... for whom nothing was too much trouble.
Even being an understudy!!

To the cast for all their hard work, patience, ideas and support.

Dawn and Laura, the twenty year wait is almost over.

# A welcome from the writer/director Alan Spence*

Dear Reader,

It is over twenty years since I started writing the play, whilst at college, and it is a sad irony that it is as relevant as when I first started.

The play had a rehearsed reading at the Live Theatre, Newcastle, in 1990, in conjunction with Northern Stage and Cleveland Theatre Company. Directed by Alisdair Ramsay, its stellar cast of local actors included: Michael Gunn, Alex Hall, Billy Fellows, Francesca Hansen, Carole Copeland and Jack Mcbride. That production was a world premiere.

Although I wrote the play before Craig Hornby's excellent 'Century of Stone', it was Craig's film that put the whole historical, social and political issues back on the agenda. The global recession and the continued problems at Redcar have only added to the poignancy of the story, a story that has been largely forgotten by the general public, both locally and nationally, being over-shadowed by the Miners' Strike 25th Anniversary and Thatcher's 30th.

What is quite unique is that wherever you meet people across Teesside, they have either been employed at British Steel, in one of the many other steel companies, or a member of their family has.

The twenty year wait has had one benefit, as I have been able to revisit the script on numerous occasions, to listen to the advice of fellow professionals and others who have read the play. The play being presented in this book is quite different from the many drafts and I am pleased to say a better piece of theatre.

Thank you for supporting this production and if you have any comments or suggestions you wish to feed back, please send them to... theatreisreallife@live.co.uk

*Best wishes,*
*Alan Spence*


\* The original version of this letter first appeared in the play programme November 2009.

# Meet the playwright... Alan Spence.

## HOW DID I GET HERE?

It was only when I was drafting a presentation for a workshop I was doing for the 2011 Middlesbrough Literary Festival, that I realised a lot of my favourite plays all had some aspect of history. I had enjoyed History at secondary school and thought it an ideal subject to study along with Drama.

So, along with Shakespeare and in no particular order: Top Girls, Road, The History Boys, Black Watch, Our Country's Good, The Pitmen Painters, Blood Brothers. Oh, What a Lovely War, Lark Rise, Murmuring Judges, Jerusalem, and The Good Hope, to name but a few, are still among my favourite plays, but does theatre actually change anything?

### EAST BARNBY

I remember coming home after my first East Barnby Drama course in 1966. I was absolutely buzzing and couldn't wait to tell me Mam all about it. Eventually, when I paused to draw breath, me Mam said, "That's the trouble with you, y'just want to be on holiday all the time."

Yet that first week as an ensemble, we had read through, rehearsed and learnt the lines of three different play extracts and performed them to an audience at a local Village Hall. Hardly a holiday but life changing nonetheless.

Mrs Bridges and Harry with everyone

On these courses, you met likeminded people who all wanted to learn, share poetry, have a laugh, perform plays and eat spam fritters. That was the other thing, they fed you three meals a day and the trick was to get on a table with girls, cos most of them didn't like spam fritters. So, all the more for us. The best spam fritters ever, courtesy of the lady in white. Mrs Bridges. She was certainly a guardian angel to us.

One year, it was Janet Cuthbert's birthday and someone had the bright idea that our band could play for the party on the Wednesday night. It would be Balthazar's second gig. Our name was taken from JP Donleavy's book, The Beastly Beatitudes of Balthazar B? No, we'd never heard of it, either but my mate John, our singer, had read it, so that became our name.

Playing live at East Barnby

Like most bands, we did covers, no originality: Beach Boys, Chuck Berry, Steppenwolf, Everly Brothers, Peter Green's Fleetwood Mac and my party piece, Cocker's With A Little Help From My Friends.

It was going really well, when some smart 'Alec' kept coming up to me, why me? Did we know 'Paranoid' by Black Sabbath? Yes, I know who it's by, I shouted. Told him, I don't know how many times and it would be the song after next. Of course, we didn't know it and the lad must have got the message.

Alan doing his best Joe Cocker

After playing for well over an hour and even doing my Cocker cameo, we got a great reception and a good night was had by all. Particularly the Birthday Girl. Bless. We were all buzzing and not ready for bed and I wanted to go for a walk, talk it through with the lad, to calm down. But no, we were all sent to our dorms. Rock 'n' roll, eh? Show biz? Who needs it? At least I didn't have to get up and go to work the next day. Only to rehearse, and that was definitely not work.

## ROAD

My first theatre trip as a Drama Teacher was to see Jim Cartwright's Road, which was organised by my Head of Department, who was covering for my actual manager on maternity leave. It was for Year 11, who had no idea what the play was about, but mind you, neither did we. But it was The Royal Court, so it should be interesting.

And it was, because it was essentially a promenade performance with the audience on the stage, mingling with the actors, who also performed all around the theatre including the circle and balcony. A number of moments remain with me.

The Professor scene, where he was surveying people's ideas and experiences, was based on real events of mass observation in 1937 in the Lancashire area, the location of Road. And when the actor playing the Professor started asking questions near our part of the stage, I answered him to keep the flow and make it look natural.

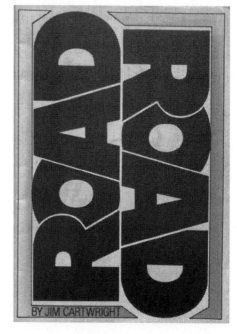

On the way home, the students ribbed me something rotten. "See Sir? He couldn't resist showing off, could he?" Everyone roared with laughter. At least they weren't complaining about the play!

The scene where Clare and Joey commit suicide. With the stage full of audience, they had to stop the performance while the bed was brought on and put in position. This took almost a minute and a half, yet as soon as the lights went down again, you were back in the world of the play, watching them die. It was riveting.

The finale when Eddie and Brink bring back Carole and Louise from the pub, and offer them 'something different'. Something different was speed drinking and listening to an Otis Redding song. "Why?" asks Carole. "We drink and listen to Otis. It stops us going mad," says Brink. And so, they all do it.

The track played is 'Try a Little Tenderness', a powerful and poignant moment, one of the few in the whole play. I couldn't believe my ears. I knew the song from the Stax Volt Tour Live album, purchased on that trip to, yes, Blankenberg in 1967. I hadn't heard it for over fifteen years. Amazing to hear it in that context.

Director Alan Clarke filmed a version of the play in 1987 which was broadcast on the BBC. I recorded it to share with students. No less powerful than the play, and filmed on location not in Lancashire, but in Easington, County Durham, which is where my mother is from. The world just got a little bit smaller. The students enjoyed it, and one lad from Tottenham said, "It's just like poetry, isn't it, Sir?" Bless Paul Thomas.

The Royal Court revived Road in 2017, directed by John Tiffany, who didn't do drama when at 6th form college, but he did all the plays, and his drama teacher gave him and Steve Hoggart (Frantic Assembly) a copy of Road to read. It changed their lives. Tiffany said, "Because we realised that plays could be about where we are from, in our voices and be poetic." This production was some thirty years after it was first performed.

The play is important to people from the North, and actor Shane Zaza said it was the first time he had read a play, where he could hear his own voice. It was a revelation. Assistant Director Grace Gummer said that plays like Road made her feel she could work in the theatre, not because of the Northern setting, but the imagination, poetry and spirit, and also the soul, something she knew and could understand.

The actor Liz White tells friends, "It's a play that was set when Britain was in the grip of Thatcher and now today, in 2017, we are in the grip of Theresa May." Tiffany was fascinated that it was written about a community that felt it couldn't get any poorer, and said, "But as a society, we have let those people down and now they are poorer than ever."

## STRATFORD UPON AVON

While Grangetown Boys' Club was a major influence on my development in terms of drama and theatre, it wasn't the only one. After leaving Eston Grange Secondary Modern with 7 Northern Examinations and Assessment Board qualifications in 1963, I enrolled on an O Level Course at a local Technical College.

Memorial Theatre, Stratford upon Avon

Four O Levels were considered to be a passport to the world, so why was I doing 7 or 8 subjects?

One of the brighter sessions at the Tech was on Wednesdays when we did something called Civics, led by an English teacher who showed us films such as Look Back in Anger, with Richard Burton and Mary Ure and directed by Tony Richardson. Not only that, he took us on a one night stay to Stratford to the Memorial Theatre and the RSC. Yes, the RSC, and all the way from Teesside.

We saw two productions. The first was Richard III with Ian Holm, Janet Suzman, Charles Kay and Peggy Ashcroft directed by Peter Hall, set in Warwick Castle, the inspiration for the set's metallic design, and Hall offered political analysis rather than lavish pageantry and spectacle.

I read in a review recently Holm's Richard, with boyish face and a naturalistic and low-key delivery resulted in an anti-heroic interpretation, well-suited to modern taste. Of course, all of that went over our heads. We knew we were watching something unique, difficult, but nonetheless very special.

The other play was a contemporary version of A Comedy of Errors, what a teacher friend would call a 'four chairs and two polo necks production', the modern dress and the comedy making that production more accessible, not better, just more accessible.

Stratford was this 15-year-old's first experience of Scrumpy Cider. Breezing into the pub behind a much cockier mate, he ordered and we drank like we knew what we were doing. But oh, the coach ride home, all 192 miles of it and no scheduled stops. Before too long my bladder was making emergency signals and was soon fit to burst. Mile after mile, my kidneys ramped up the pain factor. I have had nothing so severe since and how we made it home without a severe accident or major embarrassment is a mystery. Was someone really looking after me?

## BLACK SNOW

Keith Dewhurst's 1991 play Black Snow at the National Theatre was based on the Mikhail Bulgakov book of the same name about his time at the Moscow Arts Theatre. It had a quality cast including Ron Cook, Marion Bailey, Paul Moriarty, Gillian Barge, Peter Wight and Karl Johnson, and was directed by William Gaskill.

The play is both a critical and affectionate study of Bulgakov's time, fighting in-house censorship over his anti-Stalinist production of Moliere, with Bulgakov represented by Ron Cook's Maksudov, who goes from despair to theatrical flowering and then prompt disillusionment.

The play also includes a vicious portrait of Stanislavski in the character Vassilevich (Robin Bailey) smothered in a blanket and surrounded by sycophants, which shows how any play can be at the mercy of a director's vanity, a director who takes six weeks to rehearse a single scene, ruling out all the good spontaneous acting because of a rigid imposition of his famous Method.

In another scene, an actor is given a bike and instructed to ride it 'for love', as Stanislavski no doubt would have done, communicating his emotions through facial expressions, while circling his true love at speed, which is no mean achievement on the Cottesloe stage. What did he get from the director for his effort? Vassilevich merely clears his throat and says, "It was all wrong."

In another scene, Maksudov visits Vassilevich and is introduced to his elderly sister. "This is Mr Maksudov and he's written a play", to which the unimpressed sister replies, "But why? Aren't there enough of them already?" Hilarious, though a stark warning for anyone hoping to make their name as a playwright, as I was!

The play and production captures well the backstage bitchery and institutional politics. But some might say Bulgakov was being a little unfair to Stanislavski, whose system was developed over thirty years and based on sound techniques.

I took a Stanislavski course at the National Theatre led by Richard Hahlo who said, if you ask the current company what they thought of Stanislavski, many would say "Pardon". Yet the modern actor embraces many of the techniques and principles that Stanislavski developed: the given circumstances, the method of physical actions, subtext, the given circumstances, the magic if, objective and super-objective, to name but a few. Even though Bulgakov's play didn't last, Stanislavski's teachings have gone from strength to strength.

## GRANGETOWN BOYS' CLUB

Today some young people think they are old at thirty, but in Grangetown Boys' Club's terms, you became an 'old boy' at twenty one. This dictat may have come from some government youth service minister or memorandum. Its effect on us older members was no less telling than the big 30. Firstly, we had to take on more responsibility in the day to day running of the club, on reception and in the coffee bar, which personally I enjoyed, and with the introduction of girl members, the atmosphere changed and needed managing. But more importantly for me, anyone over 21 could not be part of productions entered for the prestigious National Boys' Cub Drama Competition and worse, I could not even attend the finals at Keele University.

What I did next, on the day of the Final, was a little out of character, trust me. I highjacked the bus (not in a violent or terrorist way... more a peaceful protest). I simply got on the bus and flatly refused to get off. Sat down in the aisle and refused to move. "I am going to support the actors," I said.

How could we have members of the club in a National Final and no one was allowed to see them? I had to go. Thankfully, people were so busy ensuring every costume, prop and more importantly the actors were safe on the coach, they seemed to forget about me. And the coach took off.

Our production was Eugene Ionesco's The Future is in Eggs and written in 1957, so quite contemporary and in the style of the Theatre of The Absurd. Neither the cast nor I had any real idea what was going on, but these plays were intended to be ironic, bring humour and a touch of lightness to an otherwise dark reality.

There were two other finalists, one a boys' club from Liverpool who did a powerful and dignified The Long, and the Short and the Tall, written by Willis Hall and originally directed by Lindsay Anderson for the Royal Court in 1958. It tells of the Japanese invasion of British Malaysia in WWII. Things go from bad to worse when the patrol radio malfunctions, and then a Japanese soldier actually stumbles upon their camp.

The other competitors were a youth club from Twickenham who offered a Greek epic, with cast filling the stage and most of the hall as the fourth wall disappeared. It was not a musical but was all 'singing and dancing', if you see what I mean? We also heard their director was a BBC man. Just how were we meant to compete?

There was a guest panel led by actor Bill Owen (yes, Compo from Last of the Summer Wine). Owen was a staunch socialist and President of the Arts for Labour Group, as well as being a big advocate of boys' club drama. Also, on the panel another actor called Violet Carson who had become a household name as Ena Sharples in Coronation Street, no less.

The Future is in Eggs tells of an arranged marriage bringing together two important families, the Jacques and the Roberts, with the requirement that they breed. Soon, both families are arguing as to who is to blame for their failure. But now the newlyweds are hungry and need to be fed. Jacques wonders why his grandfather is never heard singing anymore, only to find out he has actually passed away. Cue melodramatic emotions from the Jacques family followed by the Roberts, well they're all 'family' now of course.

It's at this point, Ionesco pulls off his coup de theatre as Grandfather Jacques comes alive and waves to one and all before joining his family, causing the audience to roar with laughter. Not only that, he wants to sing to explain how he died, but Grandmother will have none of it. Grandfather 'takes umbrage' and returns to his picture frame. Father Jacques uses the passing of Grandfather to pile pressure on the newlyweds, as they must save their race. Long live the white race is heard again and again.

After much cajoling and abuse, they produce a basket of eggs, with much congratulatory backslapping. Jacques doesn't join in these celebrations, he wants to produce Pessimists, Anarchists and Nihilists. The play includes typical Ionesco themes of failing to communicate, the pressure of conformity and a desire for a more poetic concept of life. This is shown when Jacques speaks his inner thoughts: "I want a fountain of light, incandescent water, fire of ice, snows of fire."

The actual judging was done by an independent adjudicator who talked at length and in some detail. Firstly, Grangetown Boys' Club. Our production had a minimalist set, two ramps, that rose gradually towards the back and in the centre, a large framed picture of Grandfather Jacques. Did he not like the play or even understand it any more than us?

Then Twickenham and we all thought he'd been swayed by the epic, the razzamatazz and the BBC man. We thought they must have won it. Finally, Liverpool and the fear of 'we won the war for the likes of you' mentality and then we thought they had snatched it. The adjudicator then talked about what each play required of its actors and how successful they had been in achieving the world of their play, and also the level of their performance in communicating the playwright's theatre and ideas.

There was another silence. Then the adjudicator, in an almost

throwaway style and inaudible voice said… "Grangetown have won it."
The audience did a collective, "What?" Then uproar as it finally sank in,
a momentous achievement. It was a cup final, a Littlewoods pools win,
a memory to treasure. Yes, even 54 years later. Wow.

One final comment, courtesy of Violet Carson, of whom Bill said,
"Violet really enjoyed all the plays including the Ionesco, though she
admits she didn't fully understand it, but that the eggs would come in
very handy." Oh, how we laughed.

## ANGELS IN AMERICA

The National Theatre production of Angels in America arrived in November 1993, offering a mixture of history, soap opera and myth in Tony Kusher's Gay Fantasia. It had two parts: Millennium Approaches and Perestroika, in a very minimalist setting with many actors playing two or three roles. I did find it difficult to follow, even though in my mid-40s, as we had no reference points, the world on the

edge of a Millennium, the epic problem of AIDS, when US politics
mixed with the personal lives of the characters.

The programme had a helpful list of terms, phrases and people,
a useful cross reference for the future. But as with my experience of
Shakespeare and Richard III, I knew I was watching something special,
certainly theatrical. The play alternates between history, democracy,
race, spirituality, equality, justice, freedom and love.

The cast included a twenty-five-year-old Daniel Craig playing two parts in Millennium and three parts in Perestroika before his breakthrough role in Our Friends in the North three years later. The one main memory I have of the play is a character using a hand-held smoke machine which I thought would be a great prop for a production of A Midsummer Night's Dream that I was planning.

The play has won many awards including The Pulitzer Prize, listed as part of the Western Canon major works of literature, filmed by HBO in 2003 with Al Pacino and Meryl Streep and also received many revivals such as Headlong in 2007 and the National Theatre itself in 2017 with Andrew Garfield, Nathan Lane and Denise Gough.

## RASSETT

In my third year as a student, I was once again without a school placement when my tutor, Huw Thomas, said there was a school in Wanstead needing a student and you may get a free trip to France out of it. "Where's Wanstead?" I said. "East London," said Huw. I was living in Turnpike Lane, it was gonna be a hell of a trek! Huw's prompt was a godsend as the school had proper drama spaces, a Head of Department in Don Hendy who knew what he was doing and told you at regular intervals, but I also got to go on the free trip!

The Redbridge Association of Secondary Schools English Teaching Theatre was its proper title. I didn't know any of the students and none of the content of the show, and we were to perform to both primary and secondary schools.

Our coach took us to Portsmouth for the ferry to St Malo but heavy weather delayed our departure, and when we did sail, the crossing was like a wild fairground ride. That I managed to get some sort of sleep and to retain my supper was nothing short of a moral victory. It was February and St Malo was covered in four inches of snow, as if we'd been blown off course and landed in Sweden or Norway. But this was France!

Our journey south to Chatelleraut, where Companies A and B would separate, was necessarily cautious, and our excitement was put on ice. Then crash. On a country lane, kilometres from nowhere, the last thing you would expect to see, let alone crash into was... a fully loaded car transporter. The impact smashed several windows, but thankfully no one was injured, as most were catching up on lost sleep so were out of the firing line.

We arrived for our official reception some five hours late. No time for etiquette, bonjour or au revoir, we were shoehorned into a VW minibus. There were nine bodies, as many suitcases, props, instruments et al. Arriving in Angouleme some ninety minutes later, we were shattered after thirty hours travel, and nervous of meeting our hosts. But at least there was no snow. It was then, I realised I had left my briefcase in Chatellerault, complete with the soundtrack for the show. Welcome to Theatre in Education, Mr Spence.

*"There's a tradition in British intellectual life of mocking any non-political force that gets involved in politics, especially within the sphere of the arts and the theatre."*
Harold Pinter

## MURMURING JUDGES

David Hare wrote a trilogy of plays exploring Great Britain's most hallowed institutions. The first was Racing Demon which was about the Church of England. Second was The Absence of War which examined political parties and then Murmuring Judges which looked at a single case of British justice.

The play's title refers to an 18th century arcane crime of 'scandalising the court' by criticising the judiciary, in Scotland known as 'murmuring 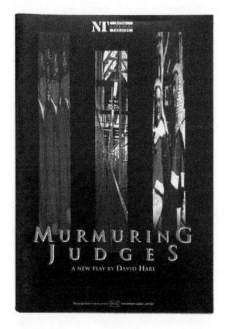 judges'. Often used to silence radicals such as John Wilkes, editor of the Birmingham Daily Argus, who described a judge as 'an impudent little man in horsehair'. The Daily Worker was also fined for describing a Conservative judge as 'a bewigged puppet exhibiting a strong class bias'.

Murmuring Judges portrays just one case of British justice: the trial, conviction and appeal process of a dubiously convicted accomplice in a theft and kidnapping attack from the view of the police, lawyers and the judiciary, as well as from inside the prison system.

The original production opened in the Cottesloe Theatre, but had transferred to the Olivier Theatre by the time we saw it. Designer Bob Crowley produced an amazing set and ideas. When a leading QC is taking a new female colleague to the opera, the back of the stage opens and a taxi arrives from which they get out and onto a rolled out red carpet. They are shown to their seats by frock-coated ushers.

Later in the play, prisoners were having a shower when a man was attacked and stabbed, totally realistic. Perhaps the most powerful moment was when the stage split in two, one side having the isolated and innocent man Gerard in his cell, while opposite was one of the many lush and indulgent banquets that lawyers must attend as part of their qualification process.

Hare examines this case from each of the sides responsible for the system in the late 1980s and early 1990s coping with increasing immigration and rising terrorism with the IRA, a problem compounded by the injustices and insensitivities of older proponents who cannot see past the traditions of British 'justice'. The play is bleak, not least for the innocent Gerard, who remains incarcerated, ravaged with despair and sexual assault, and we all know it's a set up. Will the corruption be exposed? At the end of the play, PC Sandra Bingham, played by Lesley Sharp, walks towards the audience and says, "Sir, can I have a word?"

Given the scale of this production's requirements, revivals were unlikely, and the play had a limited legacy. It received a five night run at The Old Fire Station Theatre, Oxford and was generally well received by Liam Brett of the Daily Info, Oxford. It was also performed by the Birmingham Rep in 2003, and received a four star review from the Guardian. In 2016, a Cambridge University production got four and a half stars from its Varsity magazine. Hare was himself a graduate from Cambridge so paying homage to an old boy?

## MIDDLESEX POLYTECHNIC

It may surprise some people that when trying to decide if I could write a play, I chose to make a film. At the time, it just seemed logical. I decided to do it for my Honours, so no pressure. When most of my colleagues at Middlesex Polytechnic were doing research, surveys on reading ages, behavioural groups or the teaching of science to girls, I was going to make a film… why wouldn't I?

We'd had the film lectures, learnt all about 'mise en scene', even made our own shorts, well some of us did. I helped my

Trent Park. Now part of an exclusive property development

contemporary Richard Tharp do a pop video of The Coasters' Love Potion Number Nine, and I appeared as a pointy finger. I still have a copy somewhere.

But a film? A feature film? No, not quite. In a previous module, I devised a performance with another student, using a series of facts, poems and play extracts. It was only towards the end, the audience understand and realise they were man and wife. This got me thinking… I borrowed script extracts from all over: Ann Jellicoe, Alan Bennett, Roger McGough… I even used some of my own poetry, then scripted the second half of the film.

It was the story of a relationship, over a twenty-five year period told through a seasonal structure of Spring, Summer, Autumn, Winter and then again Spring. A love story that got lost through family tragedy, a failure to communicate, a sense of being unloved and unwanted, and… life just getting in the way. The title was a mandolin instrumental by Richard Thompson, from his Strict Tempo album. I loved it and it seemed so apt.

When I told people what I was doing, they often asked, "Will we learn anything new?"

"I doubt it," I said.

What started as an experiment almost cost me my Honours. I am eternally grateful to Sarah Hupfield and Gary Stonhill, who as well as doing camera, lighting and sound, helped with auditions, getting to locations, organising me and keeping me on track and in mind and spirit. I also didn't have a car and I couldn't drive!

We needed to cast seven actors and auditioned many more, filmed in four different locations, Finsbury Park and three different student households, then there was the editing.

In Finsbury Park, we were approached by a park keeper who, seeing the camera, asked what we were doing. "Making a film," I said. "Gonna be on the telly, is it?" he enquired. "That would be nice," I said. As if it wasn't bad enough, dealing with all the additional noises of aircraft, police and ambulance sirens and the barking dogs. One wrong word and he might just have kicked us out.

Filmed on the Haringey Ladder off Green Lanes in North London, the first of our student houses included a character running down the street, and because we were using Sara and Gary rather than the actors, we had to film a bed scene focusing purely on their feet. I think it worked.

In a high-rise Edmonton flat also North London, I managed to engage two actors in a loving dance sequence, on a roof top that was viewed from the sixth floor. Very BBC Wednesday Play. It was only after several takes did I realise that in the establishing shot, you could see a SAVE THE GLC sticker which was not appropriate for the period. You have to be so careful!

In the final location of Highbury, that was the family home, we hadn't checked the fixture list and Arsenal were at home, which made parking almost impossible, to say nothing of the continuous extra noise going past the window! Finally, there was the editing.

I had never done any film editing as such, the biggest thing I had worked on was a 4 Track Grundig to record music. So, no experience therefore and I wasn't the only student or lecturer needing access to the two editing suites. Then there was the byzantine booking system. Editing was two steps forward and fourteen back. I can't believe I didn't just throw it all in the bin.

Then, a kind lecturer, seeing my plight, gave me his booking space and I sort of made it work. Don't ask me how. The film was nearly an hour long and yes, it has glitches but I think my ideas came across and I displayed a degree of craft, creativity and management skills.

My assessment came in the form of two screenings, in the Blue Room at Middlesex Polytechnic, and in the palatial former home of the

Sassoon family, whose cousin was the poet Seigfried Sassoon, rooms that would have seen visitors such as the Duke of Windsor and Mrs Simpson, Charlie Chaplin, Winston Churchill, T.E. Lawrence and Rex Whistler. I needed some of Chaplin's greatness to rub off.

While feedback was generally positive, one or two comments from lecturers helped. One lecturer said they liked how a particular scene was shot, showing invention and understanding. While another said, "It was very bitter, wasn't it?" Apart from that, no official feedback, no mark or grade. Was I trying to be too clever? How could they compare it to a Year 8 reading survey or a study of the teaching of science to girls? Is this why I got a 2:2? Not bad for a South Bank lad who had left school, over twenty years previously. I'm not bitter.

## THE MADNESS OF GEORGE III

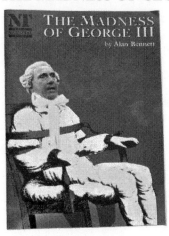

Alan Bennett wrote The Madness of George III as a screenplay though it first appeared on the National stage in 1991 and was eventually filmed in 1994, both directed by Nicholas Hytner on Bennett's insistence. It is the story of a monarch in the second part of his reign having to cope with what was perceived as mental illness and/or porphyria, an awful and unknown blood condition, to say nothing of his disloyal family and several attempts to usurp his power.

The production had superb costumes, even the minor courtiers, and the staging was every inch a Royal court against a massive set of stairs, above which was a glistening Royal blue light. Those stairs were regularly used for entrances and exits to the sound of Handel and such a glorious spectacle. Much has been written about Nigel Hawthorne's exemplary portrayal of the much misunderstood King.

Bennett and Hawthorne took the audience on an incredible emotional journey from the likeable and fair, Farmer George, who calls his wife Mrs King. But make no mistake, George III is nonetheless indisputably in charge. "I am the verb, sir, not the object," he tells a subject. Then the descent into madness. Hawthorne must spew the random gibberings of a man who has lost all control. And during his better moments, acting out King Lear, is absolute theatrical genius in more ways than one.

After its London run, the play toured the UK and the United States returning to the National Theatre in 1993. It went on to Athens and Israel. Subsequent UK productions have been a personal success for both David Haig and Mark Gatiss in 2010 and 2020, respectively. The play is an accepted classic and may have changed one or two minds about King George III, his family as well as attitudes to mental illness.

## HEAD OF DEPARTMENT

I qualified as a Drama and History Teacher in 1986, then did a part time Master's Degree in Film and Television, at the Institute of Education from 1988-1990, just as mortgage interest rates went up to 15%. This resulted in a very challenging time financially. I needed to get another job asap.

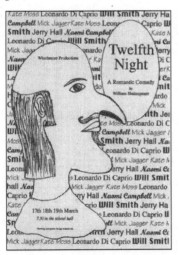

Loxford High School was a train ride from South Tottenham then a walk across Barking Park. There was always somebody exercising their Rottweiler or Doberman and they could smell my fear from 150 yards. On every occasion. Did they know I had been attacked by a dog some years earlier? It was a neighbour's dog whose name was Andy the Alsatian. I had teeth marks on my arm for weeks.

I achieved my first Head of Department role in 1991 and although I couldn't drive, the journey by bus from Tottenham to Winchmore Hill was a lot less stressful, even when surrounded by school kids.

It was a fruitful time for me, a time of valuable professional and personal development with examination groups, school productions, theatre trips and visiting companies, as well as becoming an examiner for both Drama and Media Studies.

When we were hanging the lights for our production of Romeo and Juliet, one pupil asked a friend, "Why are we not using the stage?" His friend replied, "It's one of Mr Spence's arty farty ideas." When the lights were up, another pupil said, "I get it now, Sir, the audience are going to be much closer to the actors. It will be more intimate, won't it, Sir?"

And what do we call this type of staging, I asked? Silence. It's what we call 'thrust' staging, where the performance area is out into the audience and, yes, more intimate, well said, young man.

It was during my time at Winchmore School that I began to have ideas about setting up a Youth Theatre at the school and to facilitate those ideas, I studied for a Diploma in Theatre and Education at the Central School of Speech and Drama. This was led by Chris Elwell, now Director/CEO at the Half Moon Theatre, London.

I used the final part of the course to research a range of papers and experts, and write a proposal for a theatre activity at Winchmore School, including market research. This gave a clear indication that at least forty pupils and their families were interested. This was very positive. There was even lottery money for schools that could be allocated for such projects, and a sum of £2000 was mentioned.

Cast of Cinderella Winchmore School in 1992

Our Head was a Catholic, a serving JP, and often, any ideas of productions or festivals had to serve the Christian community. Therefore, plays like Zigger Zagger were out. Yet when covering Our Country's Good with the A Level group, I was allowed to hire a full set of costumes and two antique rifles, rifles for someone to shout 'bang' for Scene 2: Punishment. It cost the school £50, and that was nearly thirty years ago!

Our Headteacher got her revenge when she bounced the Music Department and the Drama Department into a production of Fiddler on the Roof. As many will know, Fiddler requires musicians to be Grade 8 and no amount of negotiation or pleading by my colleague, the Head of Music, would shift her. We were blessed with a trio of strong student singers and a Topol, played by a laddish Greek-Cypriot 6th former, who seemed to have most of his family and friends in the audience. It turned out well.

For my youth theatre proposal, I was invited to make a presentation to the Headteacher and Governors and our Teacher Governor assured me that it would just be a formality. It turned out to be a 25-30 minute grilling, and my commitment to my own professional development, wanting to provide something for the school, to say nothing of my research, all counted for nothing.

Alan doing his bit on Red Nose Day

One of the parent governors was a solicitor who was worried about inviting the community into the school. "Don't we do that on a regular basis, and in so many ways?" I suggested. "Yes, but who will be responsible for

42

these people?" These people were going to be local youngsters whose parents would be just a phone call away, just like our own pupils.

I assured them that there would be rules and regulations regarding behaviour, and the current interest in the project meant that we would be self-sufficient at the start. Furthermore, if we were to access Lottery monies, then didn't we need to have a community commitment? Silence. Well, that was a vote of no confidence, if ever there was one.

Sir Geoff, as I used to call him ("Oh Sir Geoffrey Saved the World") after the Bee Gees song, was a well-meaning colleague, who was now red faced and couldn't apologise enough. "Alan, I never thought it would be like that," he said. "If I'd known, I would have told you not to bother." Great.

The Headteacher never mentioned it again, and so neither did I. What happened to that £2000? The Head commissioned a stained glass window at the school entrance. It is still there, nearly thirty years on. I'm not bitter! Why did they not want to give our pupils and students a real opportunity?

## THE PITMEN PAINTERS

I was rather reluctant to go and see Lee Hall's Pitmen Painters for a number of reasons. I wasn't a big fan of Billy Elliott also by Lee Hall, and both the film and the theatre production had original music by Elton John. Did it really have to be an Elton John song? The moment when Billy's dad sings his late wife's favourite song: Trimdon Grange Explosion? Close the Coalhouse Door? No talk of cultural misrepresentation here, a missed opportunity to celebrate mining culture and history? But then money doesn't talk, it screams.

A friend of mine was a dialect coach on a film called Gabriel and Me set in Newcastle, and through him I got to see a cast and crew screening. The film had a screenplay by Hall and was based on Hall's book, 'I love You Jimmy Spud'. Jimmy's grandad is dying and he believes that only the Angel Gabriel, played by Billy Connolly, can save him.

Apart from the ridiculous opening sequence filmed on a verdant Isle of Man, we are quickly back to a sink estate, a kid bullied at school and a dysfunctional family, where no one loves him. A film that could

have been emotional and life enhancing is used as a comic vehicle for Connolly, who to be fair, doesn't over-do it.

The National did a Dutch play called The Good Hope again written by Hall, about fishing vessels putting to sea in very unsafe conditions and many dying as a result. Hall set his in Whitby in 1900 and had Sutcliffe photographs in the programme that inspired set designer Hayden Griffin. Music and lyrics by John Tams and Chris Coe. What could go wrong?

Director Bill Bryden's first half offered realistic sets, combined with folk music and dancing, all adding to a feeling of time and place. The acting of the ensemble cast also gave a reality for the grimness of this kind of life. It is almost inevitable that any woman in the town will have lost at least one loved one to the sea.

The love-affair between Tom Georgeson's ship owner and Frances De La Tour's widow was too soap opera for me. Her husband and two other sons had all died at sea, her son James was the local trouble-maker wanting to change things, and yet she demanded her 17-year-old, her youngest, go to sea... this all fed my unease.

This is one of the very few plays that have actually changed anything, over nine years for Herman Heijerman's play, to get the Dutch government to outlaw practices, that has brought about the deaths of so

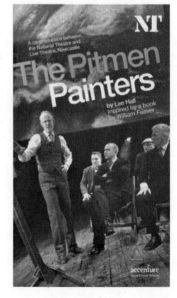

many. Could that part of story not be included, to show that theatre could actually change a country's laws?

In spite of my reservations, The Pitmen Painters was a superb production, based on William Feaver's book of the same name, telling the story of the Ashington Painters. It asks questions about education, culture and the working classes.

Accessible, funny, heart wrenching and so informative. I have seen it now three times with different friends and we all love it. It also inspired me in my own productions in the use of screens and intertitles and the importance of working class culture. There is even the Woodhorn Museum, where you can go and see all their paintings.

## TEACHER DEVELOPMENT WEEK

While at Winchmore School, I undertook a number of activities to ensure my professional and personal development: the Diploma at Central School Speech and Drama, and becoming an examiner for Drama and Media Studies. In 2000, I undertook a Teacher Development Week at The National Theatre. This was an amazing free training opportunity for Drama Teachers from both primary and secondary schools, provided by a charity, Business in the Community, and covered many aspects of theatre and production.

We met Jack Bradley the Literary Manager, we had a backstage tour and various seminars on education events and front of house and production accounts. We also attended three evening performances and yes, had our meals in the canteen, where we hobnobbed with the great and the good as they snatched sustenance between their hectic rehearsal and performance schedules.

The three productions were Battle Royal by Nick Stafford featuring Simon Russell Beale and Zoe Wanamaker, Bill Bryden's The Mysteries in a new version by Tony Harrison, and The Island by Athol Fugard with Jon Kani and Winston Ntshona in a National Theatre co-production with the Market Theatre in Johannesburg. Feeling sorry for Zoe Wannamaker as Caroline of Brunswick up against Simon Russell Beale's Prince Regent, I left at the interval. The other two productions were superb.

For our final task, we were put into groups and were required to pitch a new play idea, which would be mounted by our new 'independent company', in a co-production partnership with the National Theatre. This required us to present our ideas/pitch on the final day. The first Harry Potter book was in vogue at the time and two of our group who were primary school teachers and deeply involved with it in their classes suggested Potter as our topic. A family day at the theatre... how prophetic?

Another group went for a more adult offering, Joe Orton's The Killing of Sister George, starring Miriam Margoyles and Billy Connolly! We thought that hilarious too but it gets better. The production would have music by the Chemical Brothers. This shocked and surprised at least one member of the Education Team who said, "Given the average age of the audience (at that time), was 55 years, did they assume that the Chemical Brothers would be of interest to them?" There was a silence. Then a quiet voice from nowhere said, "I think they have an auntie works in admin?" And the whole place fell about.

## BLACK WATCH

I first learnt of Gregory Burke's Black Watch from a BBC documentary about the play, and how it all came together, with some excerpts from their performances in Scotland. The documentary blew me away, yet I felt I had very little chance to see the play as it had toured extensively all over the world.

Every viewing of that documentary, sometimes with friends, made me desperate to see this production. When the Barbican announced there would be performances from 27th November 2010 to 22nd January 2011, I was desperate for a ticket. Thankfully, a drama teacher colleague and friend were as keen as I was.

Having seen the large venues such as the Highland Showground,

I wondered how the production could be accommodated in the smaller confines of The Barbican. The National Theatre were desperate to host the play and it took a year before the Barbican was chosen. They kept the traverse staging and cut down on audience numbers. It took nothing away from the performance, and we as audience were even closer to the action.

It was back in 2004, when Vicky Featherstone as newly appointed Artistic Director and Chief Executive of the National Theatre of Scotland, asked writer Gregory Burke to monitor the amalgamation of the Black Watch, the oldest Highland regiment with other Scottish regiments.

The rest is as they say history, a history that has become intrinsically linked with that of Scotland itself. Were it not for this amazing production this could have all been lost.

An amalgamation facilitated by a Labour Government, this was one of the most prestigious fighting forces of all time, being taken out of history and subsumed, while all the time expected to support struggling Allied American forces in Iraq.

The fanfare of the Edinburgh Tattoo is totally undercut by Cammy's faltering entrance, hesitant, struggling for words, "Hey, I'm no knuckle dragger. I wanted to go and fight," and so the play within in a play begins to unfold and the inventive use of props and multi-media narrative draws you in. There is the real story, the boredom, the unexpected attacks, the heat, the letters from home, soldiers traumatised and yet sent back to fight. The media wanting to record it all, for whom? The public, politicians or both?

There is a very informative section where Cammy explains the regiment's impressive history and how those hard won victories were reflected in the changes to their uniform. All uniquely choreographed, which added another quality element to the performance.

Music was an emotional thread throughout the play, from the folk song Twa Corbies orchestrated by Davey Anderson to the bagpipes played by one of the cast and on towards the climax, Max Richter's superb November. The ensemble company left the audience in no doubt how the Black Watch had fought and fought, again and again, and won. Only to be taken down, by yet another Government decision.

*"Britain is famous for three female directors,*
*there's one who's a lesbian,*
*there's Joan Littlewood and she's retired,*
*and there's Buzz Goodbody and she committed suicide.*
*Which one are you?"*
Jude Kelly.
(The Drama School reaction to Jude wanting to be a theatre director)


## HOW DID I GET HERE?

I asked this question at the start of this chapter. I hope I have gone some way into answering that question, with the range of stories and experiences and how I became shaped by those experiences. Moving from the industrial Teesside to the classrooms of North London, to be a trustee of an Inclusive Theatre Company, setting up my own theatre company, and becoming a member of the Writers' Guild Theatre Committee and now a published playwright.

As to the supplementary question, does theatre actually change anything? Jim Cartwright's Road clearly resonates with actors, directors, audiences and students, and over thirty years later remains a key play in the theatrical canon. Something you could never say about Black Snow, but then, Bulgakov's legacy is outshone by the very man Stanislavski that he tried to criticise and down grade.

Did Angels in America help to bring understanding and humanity for the suffering of AIDs and HIV communities? Or was it only ever a fantastical piece of theatre in its narrative and the manner it told its story? Thankfully, society and medical science have both caught up and are now able to support in many ways and humanity is the better for it.

The fact that David Hare's Murmuring Judges play focuses on just one example of criminal corruption while exploring the justice system, does that detract from his central message? A justice system that had not changed since No Irish, No Blacks, No Dogs notices were common place.

Thirty years on has anything changed? There are still concerns over police numbers and with terrorism uppermost in many people's mind, report after report criticising police forces, not least the Metropolitan, and accusations of 'Lefty Lawyers' and the appalling Police and Crimes Bill to outlaw peaceful public protest. A bill that mentions statues eight times and women not once. And I haven't even mentioned Black Lives Matter... what would that play look like?

George III has often been portrayed in children's history books as 'the mad king who lost America', surely something that would be revised these days? Yet in the recent musical Hamilton, he is portrayed as a pompous sovereign. BBC's Lucy Worsley says modern historians have put his madness down to the physical, genetic blood disorder called porphyria, its symptoms including aches and pains, as well as blue urine.

That theory certainly formed the basis of Bennett's play, however, a new research project at St George's, University of London has concluded that George III did actually suffer from mental illness after all, and that research will feature in Worsley's BBC programme Fit to Rule, being broadcast on BBC 2.

Mentally ill or not, George's 60-year reign was one of success, in an increasingly industrial landscape, and prosperity, despite the loss of The Colonies, shifting the role of the monarchy from aggressive leadership to background stability. Bennett's piece has been equally successful as theatre, a film and even as a book, getting many four and five star reviews.

Theatre critic Mark Lawson suggests that Bennett's play has deepened with time, from the enjoyable history lesson that lacked wider resonance, it has proven to be prophetic and topical. Soon afterwards, the former US president Ronald Reagan revealed a diagnosis of Alzheimer's, and François Mitterrand was terminally ill, with the Élysée Palace releasing false medical bulletins, as Windsor Castle did about George III. And we learn ever more about the concealment of Winston Churchill's infirmities.

Do voters still demand leaders to be superhuman? In his article, Lawson discusses how commentators speculate freely about whether Donald Trump is insane, or if Theresa May's type 1 diabetes might affect her stamina, to say nothing of Biden's intention to run in 2024. George III partly seems a play about information management by the state, as the intrigue involves keeping a vulnerable government in power.

Yet, is Lawson guilty himself of overstating the case on short periods of mental illness? George III had a sixty-year reign that was successful in many ways, not least for outwitting the many that tried to prove him unfit.

The Pitmen Painters play had a simple and powerful message: art is for everybody. It is such a universal and obvious message, both hilarious and emotional in its telling and one that resonates with every audience that I was in. Backed by the miners themselves and the provenance of their outstanding art work, it was job done. That was missing in Hall's play The Good Hope, yet the original Dutch play was one of the very few that have changed its country's laws... why was that not celebrated? Bryden's production chose to focus on a realistic re-telling of that tragedy, shifting the location to Whitby, with a powerful seafaring community and tradition of its own. Fine, but to ignore what the original play had achieved, is in my opinion a mistake. Whether that decision lies with Bryden, Hall or both, it is theatre's loss.

The same could be said of Black Watch though for completely different reasons, as the regiment was already under review and only a sharp-eyed Vicky Featherstone picked on its significance, without which the play wouldn't exist at all. Black Watch won 22 awards between 2006 and 2009, that included two international awards, and four of the 2009 Olivier awards. It played Los Angeles and New York, Australia and New Zealand. It was still wowing audiences when I saw it in 2011. In 2016, the play celebrated its 10th anniversary. How many plays do that at home, let alone across the globe? Ask Sean Connery, Hugh Jackman and the Coen Brothers who all raved about it.

The National Theatre of Scotland's director of external affairs, Roberta Doyle, said thousands of real military personnel had watched the play around the world and gave the most moving feedback. The feedback from real soldiers was that the play 'gave them a voice, that they had never had before'. Now that's what theatre can do and has been doing for a long time.

# NOWT LIKE THIS IN AMERICA

## How it came about

The title of the play comes from a saying used by a good friend Norman Willey, a former shop steward on the Redcar Blast Furnace who used to remind us whenever we looked on the many fantastic landscapes of Teesside, that if you believe America has the best and worst of everything, Norman would always say... "Y'know, they've got nowt like this in America."

Norman saved many a press cutting from the strike and time after time got sick of me crowing about how I was going to write a play about our experiences. One day, he gave me the folder and said, "Go on then, get on with it. Write your bloody play."

The play had a rehearsed reading as part of a Live Theatre event by New Writing North in 1990, in association with Cleveland Theatre Company. Directed by Alisdair Ramsay, it had a stellar cast that included Michael Gunn, Alex Hall, Billy Fellowes, Francesca Hansen, Jack McBride and Carole Copeland.

# PART 2: THE PLAY
# NOWT LIKE THIS IN AMERICA

Synopsis:

The play is set in Eston and the BSC Redcar Complex just prior to the 1980 Steel Strike, and centres around Shop Steward John Wilkinson and his family. When a planned holiday to America is shelved because of the strike, things go from bad to worse. If John thought he had a fight on his hands at work, at home family life became nothing short of dysfunctional.

Slides are used to provide a local, national and historical perspective.

### Script notes

[-] Means a character doesn't speak.
/ Means the next character speaks.
*(Beat)* Means a change of subject/thought.

# NOWT LIKE THIS IN AMERICA

## by Alan Spence

Characters in order of appearance.

### THE WILKINSON FAMILY
Susan: *(daughter) 15, and at Secondary School.*
Maureen: *(mother) 36, not working at the moment. Housewife.*
Billy: *(son) 10, and at Primary School.*
John: *(father) 38, electrician, Shop Steward*
*on (RCO) Redcar Coke Ovens.*

### AT THE WORKS
Tony Simpson: *(boilermaker) 23, and member of Young Socialists.*
Mick Evans: *(electrician) 45, married, friend of John.*
Jeff Stanforth: *(labourer) 33, married, jack–the-lad, likes a drink.*
Dick Graham: *(engineer) 51, ex Shop Steward.*

### FAMILY FRIENDS
Sheila Wallace: *early 40s, works as a cleaner,*
*good friends with Maureen, married to Brian.*
Wendy Martin: *29, married to Peter,*
*old fashioned values and a little innocent.*
Brian Wallace: *early 40s, Married to Sheila. Electrician on RCO.*
Peter Martin: *36, Production Manager at ICI Wilton.*

*All other voices / parts played by the company.*

# ACT I

**SLIDE 1:** Nowt like this in America by Alan Spence

**SLIDE 2:** *"Trade union power in the UK interferes with market forces, causing inflation, and has to be checked, to restore the 'profitability' of the UK. I and others also believe it necessary to check union power in the aftermath of the fall of the Heath government, in the face of the 1974 strikes."*
Nicholas Ridley MP, The Ridley Report, 1977.

**SOUND:** Cavalleria Rusticana music floats in the background.

**SLIDE 3:** In 1850, John Vaughan discovers ironstone at Eston.

In 1851, the first blast furnace is blown in.

By 1861, over forty furnaces on Teesside.

**SLIDE 4:** *"This remarkable place, the youngest child of England's enterprise, is an infant, but if an infant, an infant Hercules."*
W.E. Gladstone, Middlesbrough, 1862.

**SLIDE 5:** *"The story, the marvellous story, of its rise. The idea symbolised by its history, is force – a physical, mental and moral force."*

| **SLIDE 6:** | *"Which enables communities to wrestle with, and overcome obstacles, which circumstances cast in their way. As they struggle upwards and onwards, to a better state of living."* |
| | Joseph Cowans, Middlesbrough Jubilee, 1881. |

**SLIDE 7:**  August 1979.

**LIGHTING:**  Fade up. Interior. The Wilkinson's.
Late afternoon.

**ACT 1 SC1:**  The music continues to build and we see
SUSAN WILKINSON, aged 15 moving /
conducting the music, in a world of her own.
A woman appears, MAUREEN WILKINSON,
aged 36, her Mam.

*MAUREEN puts down her bags and enters.*

**MAUR:**  Susan, Susan!! Don't you know your father's
in bed?

*MAUREEN goes and turns the music down.*

**SUSAN:**  Sorry. / Didn't see you there.

**MAUR:**  Shift relief. Nights tonight, and tomorrow.

**SUSAN:**  On his birthday?

**MAUR:**  Can't always choose y'days off. Seen our Billy?

**SUSAN:**  Yes, but he went straight out again.

| MAUR: | If he's playing football again, I'll hit him so hard he won't know whether it's Shrove Tuesday or Sheffield Wednesday. *(She notices the table)* Thanks for setting the table, luv. Look what I've got for y'Dad. |

*She exits and returns with a cake.*

| MAUR: | What d'y'think? |

| SUSAN: | One candle? |

| MAUR: | He'd be upset if we didn't get him a cake, even more, if we put the right number of candles on. |

*They both laugh.*

| SUSAN: | I got a card and signed it of course… just in case. |

| MAUR: | If he doesn't show soon, he's for the high jump. |

*They put the card at John's place.*

*Enter BILLY WILKINSON, aged 11, with a card in his hand.*

| BILLY: | Hi Mam! |

| MAUR: | Shh!! *(whispering)* Where the hell have you been? |

| BILLY: | Been to get me Dad a card. |

*MAUREEN and SUSAN are gob-smacked.*

| | |
|---|---|
| **MAUR:** | Right. Well go and wash now and don't wake your dad. *(BILLY Exits)* Y'know, if he wasn't so much like his Dad, he wouldn't last five minutes round here. |

*Enter JOHN WILKINSON half awake.*

| | |
|---|---|
| **JOHN:** | Mam! You shouldn't have bothered… |
| **MAUR:** | Sorry love, I was going to give you another fifteen minutes. |

*MAUREEN kisses his cheek.*

| | |
|---|---|
| **JOHN:** | I was being serenaded, wasn't I, Susan? |
| **SUSAN:** | Sorry, Dad. |

*SUSAN offers a chair to JOHN. He sits down.*

| | |
|---|---|
| **MAUR:** | Susan, make some tea, luv; the kettle should've boiled. |

*SUSAN goes and BILLY returns.*

| | |
|---|---|
| **BILLY:** | Happy birthday Dad!! |
| **JOHN:** | Hello son… thank you. |
| **BILLY:** | Have you seen me card yet, Dad? |
| **MAUR:** | When we're all at the table… Did you wash? |
| **BILLY:** | Yes. *(He offers his hands)* |

*SUSAN brings in tea and puts it on the table.*

**BILLY:**          Can I have some Coke?

**JOHN:**          Please?

**BILLY:**          Please!

*BILLY pours himself a drink, leaving the bottle on the table. JOHN looks and he puts the bottle on the floor.*

**JOHN:**          Who's going to say grace?

*There is a short pause.*

**ALL:**          Grace!!

*They all laugh.*

**JOHN:**          And Billy, it's not a race.

*He opens BILLY's card; it has footballers on. He reads it.*

**JOHN:**          Thanks, Billy. Want to go to see the Boro on Saturday?

**BILLY:**          Can we, Dad? Please?

**JOHN:**          We'll see.

*He opens SUSAN's card; it's got boats on.*

**JOHN:**          Oh, thanks luv.

*She kisses him and gives him the album, as his present.*

*The one she has been playing.*

**JOHN:**     What have I done to deserve this? *(He reads)* Beethoven, Elgar and Mascagni, so that's what I was listening to?

**SUSAN:**     Sorry, Dad…

**BILLY:**     I wanted to buy you Abba.

**SUSAN:**     Y'supposed to buy them something they like.

**BILLY:**     You chose it, not me.

**JOHN:**     That's enough, Billy. It's a lovely surprise, Susan, thank you both.

*He reads MAUREEN's card and they exchange smiles.*

**BILLY:**     How many kisses, Dad?

**SUSAN:**     Don't be rude!

**BILLY:**     *(Whispers)* You didn't even wrap it up!

**MAUR:**     Haven't got you anything yet, luv.

**JOHN:**     I know, it's difficult. The man who has everything.

*JOHN puts his hand out and touches MAUREEN's.*

**MAUR:**     There are still one or two sales on, we might pick up a bargain on Saturday.

**JOHN:**          Just remember, pet… no socks please,
                   we're British!

*BILLY doesn't get the joke and SUSAN groans.*

**SUSAN:**         Dad?

*Silence. BILLY is nodding his head for all he is worth,
to get SUSAN to speak up.*

**SUSAN:**         Dad-dy…

**BILLY:**         What she is trying to say is are we going to
                   America or what?

**SUSAN:**         Can you just shut!!

**JOHN:**          Can you two stop squabbling? *(He puts his knife
                   down and thinks)* Well, Mam and I have thought
                   about it carefully and at length.

**BILLY:**         We're not gonna go, are we?

**SUSAN:**         Shush, will y'?

**JOHN:**          *(He continues)* The cost of everything,
                   what we can afford, what we can save…
                   or just go to Benidorm again?

**SUSAN:**         Oh please? You promised…

**JOHN:**          It is… an awful lot of money.

**BILLY:**         I told you, didn't I?

JOHN:              So, we'd better put down a deposit on Saturday!!

*BILLY and SUSAN didn't believe what they heard,*
*don't react and then uproar.*

SUSAN:             And can we go to Disneyland?

BILLY:             And the NASA Space Station!!

JOHN:              You'll have to pull your weight and help around
                   the house or we won't be going anywhere!

*SUSAN and BILLY are full of promises,*
*much to JOHN and Maureen's amusement.*

SOUND:             Reasons To Be Cheerful, Part 3 –
                   Ian Dury and The Blockheads.

LIGHTING:          Fade down.

| | |
|---|---|
| **SLIDE 8:** | The Ridley Report on Nationalised Industries 1977.<br>Regulate wages and buy off powerful groups.<br>State powers used to break strikes.<br>A large mobile police force to stop picketing.<br>Vulnerable groups identified as Railway, Civil Service and the Steel Industry.<br>The report only came to light when leaked to The Economist in 1978. |
| **LIGHTING:** | Fade up. Coke Ovens. Locker room.<br>Early morning. |
| **SOUND:** | Fade off music. |
| **ACT I Sc II:** | **Coke Ovens. Locker room.**<br>**JEFF STANFORTH 30s, a labourer,**<br>**is reading The Sun.**<br>**MICK EVANS 40s, electrician, drinks tea.** |
| **JEFF:** | Eh! Listen to this… "Dear Claire Rayner, my father died nearly eighteen months ago, and I now have bouts of depression, even tears. I am nineteen and male, is there anything wrong with me?" What is the bloody country coming to? |

*Silence.*

| | |
|---|---|
| **MICK:** | When my father died… about three weeks afterwards, I just broke down and cried, I couldn't stop. Couldn't stop for ten to fifteen minutes. It was only then that I realised; he would never beat me again. |
| **JEFF:** | Bloody hell, Mick… Y'never said… |

| | |
|---|---|
| **MICK:** | I took our Andrew back to Catterick, and just before we left, he gave me a big hug. I couldn't handle it. Why? I love him. *(Pause)* What does Auntie Clare say then? |
| **JEFF:** | Oh, it's all normal and he must have had a good relationship with his father. We're breeding a load of bloody poofters, if you ask me. |
| **V.O:** | Gaffers coming. |
| **JEFF:** | Fucking hell!! *(He makes a quick exit)* |

*Enter TONY SIMPSON mid 20s, boilermaker, with a BSC Breakfast.*

| | |
|---|---|
| **TONY:** | Works every time… |
| **MICK:** | Still playing Russian Roulette with the canteen then? |
| **TONY:** | Best meal of the day, man. |

*JEFF returns.*

| | |
|---|---|
| **TONY:** | Got y'quicker than a Hartlepool Cod, Jeff. You losing it? |
| **JEFF:** | Y'don't get five minutes peace in here, as it is. |
| **TONY:** | You wouldn't be much use in the Revolution, comrade. |
| **JEFF:** | An' don't comrade me. Y'have as much chance of getting a revolution in this country, as Scargill getting a Knighthood. |

MICK:              Let's face it, Labour MPs are a more endangered
                   species than the blue whale.

*Enter JOHN covered in coke dust.*

JEFF:              Even shop stewards aren't safe these days,
                   eh John?

TONY:              Where y' working?

JOHN:              Dolls House. Fifth floor. Give us a hand, will y'?

TONY:              Er… I'd love to, / but…

JOHN:              I know… job requires a tradesman
                   and you're a boilermaker.

JEFF:              Only on his mother's side though.

MICK:              Cards at dinner time, John?

JOHN:              Sorry, got a Health and Safety meeting at 12.30.

MICK:              Hope y'goin to tell them we'd like some?

JOHN:              Exactly! Do us a favour, Mick, and finish it
                   for us, would'ya? I'm sure I got it to keep me
                   out of the meeting.

MICK:              Much to do?

JOHN:              Cables to connect, it's all in place,
                   tools on the job.

| | |
|---|---|
| **JEFF:** | Bit risky, John, you don't know what you might lose? |
| **TONY:** | Why? You working up there? |
| **MICK:** | Yeah, alright John, but don't forget you owe me one? |
| **JOHN:** | Cheers, Mick. Hope I can get this shite off and be human again. |

*He exits.*

| | |
|---|---|
| **JEFF:** | Tony, what did you mean? Why are you working up there? |
| **TONY:** | Don't ask me… Fagin. |

*TONY flicks food at JEFF and escapes. JEFF responds.*

| | |
|---|---|
| **JEFF:** | I'll fucking Fagin y', y' cheeky bastard. |
| **MICK:** | Children please. |
| **V.O:** | There's people trying to get to sleep, in here. |
| **SOUND:** | Money – Pink Floyd. |
| **LIGHTING:** | Fade down. |

| | |
|---|---|
| **SLIDE 9:** | *"Because of poor prices, we are withdrawing £2 million worth of orders from the export market, and the elimination of around 10,000 jobs."* Gordon Sambrook, BSC Chief of Sales, 3rd November 1979. |
| **SLIDE 10:** | *"3,500 JOBS TO GO AS AXE FALLS IN TWO WELSH TOWNS. Workforce to be cut by 25% unions told".* Western Mail, Cardiff, 23rd November 1979. |
| **LIGHTING:** | Fade up. Internal. The Wilkinson's. |
| **SOUND:** | Fade off music. |
| **ACT I Sc III:** | **BILLY and SUSAN are outside the bathroom; BILLY is counting his money. SUSAN is not impressed.** |
| **BILLY:** | 10, 11, 12… that's £13. |
| **SUSAN:** | How many more times? |
| **BILLY:** | I've had a lot of expense recently. |
| **SUSAN:** | The Boro? That's not an expense, that's a liability. |
| **BILLY:** | Who's a liar? Anyways… I don't get as much pocket money as you… 16, 18, 20… so that's £13.20. How much have you saved? |
| **SUSAN:** | Oh pounds!! |

*She goes in the bathroom.*

**BILLY:** As much as me? An' hurry up!!

**SUSAN:** *(Shouts)* An' I'll have even more with me part-time job.

**BILLY:** Part time job? Y'never out the bathroom. *(Pause)* I really need to go. Are y'gonna be long?

**SUSAN:** Making myself even more beautiful / than ever.

**BILLY:** Don't think I can wait that long.

**SUSAN:** *(Pops her head out)* Well y'd better start wearing Pampers, otherwise we won't be going to Florida!!

**BILLY:** How long y' gonna be? It's not like anyone would wanna take you out!!

**SUSAN:** You just concentrate on saving y'money and sorting y'plumbing out. Don't want to be going to Disneyland with no bedwetter, do I?

**BILLY:** *(He laughs)* Well, Ian says we won't be going to America cos there's going to be a strike.

**SUSAN:** *(Shouts)* Who?

**BILLY:** His dad's a manager down Redcar Complex. Said no one's gonna have any money *(Beat)* There'll be trouble if I do a mess…

*Enter SUSAN with a towel round her head.*

**SUSAN:** How come you know so much
and not be potty-trained?

*SUSAN pulls a face as if she smells something.*

**BILLY:** Gotcha!!! *(Laughs)* Works a treat every time!!

*BILLY swans in to the bathroom. SUSAN screams as she exits.*

**SUSAN:** *(Shouts)* Bet y'forgotten Christmas pressies?

**BILLY:** *(Appears at the door)* Not me, all sorted.
*(He counts again)* 1, 2, 3…

**SOUND:** I Have A Dream – Abba.

**LIGHTING:** Fade down.

| | |
|---|---|
| **SLIDE 11:** | BSC DEMANDS 10,000 REDUDANCIES.<br>An offer of 2%, can increase to 4%<br>in self-financing deals.<br>Inflation 17.4%.<br>Steel House, Grosvenor Place, London,<br>3rd December 1979. |
| **SLIDE 12:** | *"UNION BULLIES TAKE A BASHING"*<br>The Sun, 8th December 1979. |
| **LIGHTING:** | Fade up. Internal. Christmas Day. Lunch time. |
| **SOUND:** | Fade off. |
| **ACT 1 Sc IV:** | **Christmas Day at the Coke Ovens.**<br>**MICK and JOHN talk.** |
| **MICK:** | Y'don't regret it then? Giving up the steward's job? |
| **JOHN:** | Nah!! All they want is someone who'll moan to the gaffer then vote themselves half a day's strike so they can go to the Club. Now we've got a real fight on our hands, first National Strike in 28 years!! What do they do? Work all the hours God sends doing safety cover!! *(Pause)* And the bloody papers are screaming 'militant' this and 'bully boy' that. Y'couldn't get this lot out of the gate, if Sylvia Kristel was standing there, with a blank cheque between, between / her… |
| **MICK:** | Teeth!! *(Beat)* If there's safety cover, won't that help to save jobs? |

*Silence.*

| | |
|---|---|
| **JOHN:** | You weren't at the meeting? |
| **MICK:** | They also believe if the strike gets them a rise then even better. Y'can't argue with democracy, John. |
| **JOHN:** | Is that what you call it? *(Beat)* And if you don't mind me asking? |

*Silence.*

| | |
|---|---|
| **MICK:** | I'll be striking, don't you worry. |
| **JOHN:** | *(He smiles)* … I thought so. |

*Enter TONY, much the worse for drink.*

| | |
|---|---|
| **TONY:** | Oh no, I don't know if I need a shit, shave or a haircut! |
| **MICK:** | You've been on them Drambuie shandies again, haven't y? |
| **TONY:** | How can I feel this bad and still be alive? |
| **MICK:** | What you need is BSC breakfast inside y'. |

*TONY is only just hanging on…*

| | |
|---|---|
| **JOHN:** | Mick, it's Christmas Day, gotta be turkey and all the trimmings!! |

*TONY wretches and is almost sick.*

| | |
|---|---|
| **TONY:** | Will you two give over!! |

*MICK and JOHN stand and become a 'double act'.*

**MICK:**　　　　We're having the in-laws this year.

**JOHN:**　　　　Makes a change from turkey.

**MICK:**　　　　I wouldn't say my father- in-law was intelligent…

**JOHN:**　　　　But he thought the Red Arrows was a Russian darts team.

*TONY groans again and leaves.*

**JOHN:**　　　　What would the comrades say if they saw him like this?

**MICK:**　　　　What's bloody Dick going to say more-like?

**JOHN:**　　　　He could rub dust on his hands and pretend he's been busy!!

*They both laugh, like a couple of school kids.*
*Enter DICK GRAHAM, shift engineer, and the mood changes.*

**BOTH:**　　　　Merry Christmas… Boss!!

**DICK:**　　　　Yeah, cheers lads. It's alright for some.
　　　　　　　　Who's staying all day?

**MICK:**　　　　Tony and Jeff.

**DICK:**　　　　Seen either of them?

**JOHN:**　　　　They were here… a moment ago.

| | |
|---|---|
| **DICK:** | Tell them No. 2 Screen's shed tiles, spillage everywhere. |
| **MICK:** | Consider it done. |

*DICK exits.*

| | |
|---|---|
| **JEFF:** | *(Creeping back in)* Has he gone? |
| **MICK:** | Yes. But the good news is… y'got a job. |
| **JEFF:** | On Christmas Day? |
| **MICK:** | Y'did volunteer. |
| **JEFF:** | Still thought I'd get a few bevies in the Club. It's traditional! |
| **JOHN:** | Have a guess? *(Pause)* No. 2 Screen. |
| **JEFF:** | Again? Why don't they just rebuild it? I'm not offering, mind. And where's my mate? |
| **MICK:** | Crawled in a corner to die. |
| **JEFF:** | He bloody will if I get me hands on 'im. I've missed the kids and their prezzies. |
| **JOHN:** | What did you get the little darlings this year? Or didn't your lass tell y'? |
| **JEFF:** | Now, I'm gonna miss the fucking Club. |
| **JOHN:** | Time to go, Mick, Santa awaits! |

*JOHN and MICK exit. Enter TONY still looking the worse for wear.*

**JEFF:**          Oh my God! It's… Dorian Grey? *(Pause)* Look…
I'll get the gear, you just concentrate on not
chucking up!! *(Pause)*

*JEFF exits followed by TONY who is heard retching.*

**JEFF:**          *(Shouts)* Christ, it's enough to turn y'heathen.

**SOUND:**      Oh Come All Ye Faithful.

**LIGHTING:**   Fade down.

**SLIDE 13:**       *"Some 5,500 to lose jobs at Corby,*
                    *when steelmaking is phased out and*
                    *will receive £27,000 in redundancy."*
                    Daily Mail, 28th December.

**SLIDE 14:**       *"WAGES ARE SECONDARY TO KEEPING*
                    *THE PLANT OPEN, AND SECURING OUR*
                    *FUTURE"*
                    Craft Union Official, The Sun, 29th December.

**SLIDE 15:**       *"THE STEEL FIRES ARE GOING OUT"*
                    Evening Gazette, 29th December.

**LIGHTING:**       Lights Up. Internal. The Wilkinson's Evening.

**SOUND:**          Fade off.

**ACT I Sc V:**     **New Year's Eve. BILLY on the settee, bored.**

*Enter MAUREEN, she's been cooking.*

**MAUR:**           I thought you were here to help?

**BILLY:**          You haven't given me a job yet!

**MAUR:**           I said tidy in here, then get ready. Put your new
                    jumper on.

**BILLY:**          Do I have to?

**MAUR:**           Go on, I'll do in here now.

*BILLY exits. MAUREEN tidies up.*

*Enter SHEILA WALLACE, early 40s, neighbour and best friend of MAUREEN's. She too is warm from the kitchen.*

**SHEILA:** That's the last of the sausage rolls…

**MAUR:** Oh, thanks, Sheila, you've been a great help.

**SHEILA:** Is y'Mam coming over?

**MAUR:** No. Her and a friend are in Scarborough.

**SHEILA:** And she didn't invite us?

**MAUR:** Booked a festive package for New Year – all in. Hope she'll be okay.

**SHEILA:** Is she still missing your Dad?

**MAUR:** Yeah. Perhaps, she's trying to move on.

**SHEILA:** I hope so… can't be easy. Not at this time of the year. And Susan?

**MAUR:** Round her mates, she'll be here at some point.

**SHEILA:** Like Wendy… planning one of her grand entrances, no doubt.

**MAUR:** Check our Billy is finished; you freshen up and I'll pour us a drink.

*SHEILA exits, MAUREEN goes to the kitchen. BILLY returns, he's got his Xmas jumper on, and a grumpy face.*

**BILLY:** Mam… can I have a drink?

**MAUR:** *(From the kitchen)* Aye luv.

*BILLY sits on the settee; MAUREEN comes in with an orange for BILLY.*

**BILLY:** Can't I have a proper drink?

**MAUR:** This is a proper drink for an 11-year-old.

**BILLY:** I was thinking beer, whiskey? / It is New Year's Eve.

**MAUR:** Think again, Billy, one drink will lead to another and y'won't last five minutes. Just like your Dad!!

**BILLY:** [-]

**MAUR:** Y'don't want to miss the party?

*Enter SHEILA ready for action…*

**SHEILA:** That's better. Ooo' thanks!! *(She takes her drink)* Mind you, this could be the last party for a while. John will be striking, no doubt?

**MAUR:** He's always prided himself in being his own man. Still, we may's well be skint, as 'ave nowt, eh?

**BILLY:** *(Whispers)* Bloody adults. *(BILLY reluctantly sips his orange)*

**SOUND:** Doorbell rings.

**SHEILA:** Wendy?

**MAUR:** Not before time! *(She goes to let her in, greetings are heard)*

*Enter WENDY MARTIN, 29 years, another neighbour*
*and dressed to the nines.*

**SHEILA:** Hi'ya Wendy, where y'off to? State Opening of Parliament?

**WENDY:** A bit early with the Angostura, aren't we, Sheila? Even for you?

**SHEILA:** Give over, y'softie, y'look great. Give us y'coat. *(She takes her coat and exits)*

*MAUREEN returns giving WENDY a look.*

**MAUR:** And what else did we get for Xmas? You make Sheila and me look like, like... the Ugly Sisters.

*Enter SHEILA...*

**SHEILA:** Eeeya! Oo, you calling a sister, then?

*They both laugh.*

**MAUR:** Sorry, Wendy, what would you like to drink, luv?

**WENDY:** A chilled Blue Nun if you have it, please?

**MAUR:** We want for now't, we've got. I'n't that right, Sheila?

*WENDY takes her place next to BILLY on the settee.*

**WENDY:** And what did Father Christmas bring you then, Billy?

| | |
|---|---|
| **BILLY:** | Y'don't still believe in him, do y'? Me Mam and Dad buy all our presents. Bloody grown-ups!! |

*MAUREEN returns with more drinks.*

| | |
|---|---|
| **MAUR:** | Here Sheila, Wendy. *(Raising her glass)* The night is but young… |

| | |
|---|---|
| **ALL:** | Cheers!! |

*SHEILA and MAUREEN take a good swig, while WENDY sips.*

| | |
|---|---|
| **BILLY:** | Mam, can I have…? |
| **MAUR:** | No y'can't. |
| **BILLY:** | Dad would let me… |
| **MAUR:** | Y'Dad's not here. |
| **BILLY:** | I hope I never grow up!! |
| **MAUR:** | Billy, y'might not get the chance. *(Pause)* Look, why don't y'get ready and be our DJ! Yeah?!! |
| **BILLY:** | Can I play Abba? |
| **MAUR:** | Yeah… but not straight away, eh? |
| **WENDY:** | Shouldn't they be back by now? It's 11.45! |
| **MAUR:** | They've probably invited the whole pub. |
| **WENDY:** | This is the first New Year's Eve I have not been out with Peter. |

**SHEILA:** Well, y'not too old for a change then, eh?

**WENDY:** The Labour Club, good friendly crowd. You know, they even keep us tickets! Every year! *(She looks out the window).*

**SHEILA:** *(Whispers to MAUREEN)* Can y'imagine, if she turned up at the Club dressed like that?

**MAUR:** They'd probably think she was the cabaret.

**SHEILA:** She is, isn't she? *(They laugh)*

**MAUR:** Ee don't make me laugh, me lips are chapped.

**SOUND:** Voices can be heard and get louder. They are doing The Conga.

**WENDY:** No… they're doing The Conga already!!

**SHEILA:** Fasten y'seat belts girls, it's going to be a bumpy ride!!

*Enter JOHN, BRIAN WALLACE, Sheila's husband and PETER MARTIN, Wendy's husband, all covered in Christmas Party paraphernalia.*

**MAUR:** I thought y'were bringing people back?

**JOHN:** *(JOHN turns to speaks to an invisible group)* Okay everyone, this is Maureen and Maureen, this is everyone!

| | |
|---|---|
| **MAUR:** | Are you listening to me? Sheila and I have put in a good shift here, so you could go and enjoy yourself. It had better not go to waste! |
| **JOHN:** | Don't worry, if everyone Peter invited turns up, y'gonna need five loaves and two fishes. *(Beat)* Is the telly on? Don't want to miss Auld Lang Syne. *(He goes to check)* |
| **WENDY:** | *(Quietly to PETER)* What's he talkin' about? Five loaves and two fishes? And y'got all lipstick on'y!! |
| **PETER:** | Not as much as you. *(Beat)* Any chance of a drink? |
| **WENDY:** | Can we just slow down a bit? All these people that you've invited, are they friends of yours? |
| **PETER:** | Not all of them... it's New Year's Eve. Remember?! |
| **WENDY:** | I probably won't know any of them. *(PETER doesn't respond)* We should have gone to the Labour Club. It's our tradition. |
| **PETER:** | Who's stopping y'? Want a top up? |

*PETER disappears and WENDY is not pleased...*

| | |
|---|---|
| **JOHN:** | Billy, have you been messing with these plugs? |
| **BILLY:** | Mam said I could be DJ. |
| **JOHN:** | Let's have the telly on, for Auld Lang Syne. |

| | |
|---|---|
| **BILLY:** | Oh, bloody adults. |
| **JOHN:** | Has Mam been giving you drink? |

*JOHN rearranges the plugs and puts the telly on.*

| | |
|---|---|
| **BRIAN:** | *(In his best Bogart)* Haven't I seen you somewhere before? |
| **SHEILA:** | Possibly… |
| **BRIAN:** | Tangiers? |
| **SHEILA:** | I doubt it. |
| **BRIAN:** | Must be the Labour Club then, eh? |
| **SHEILA:** | I don't want to put you off y'stride, Bogart… but your flies are open!! |
| **BRIAN:** | Oh, the not, are the? |
| **SHEILA:** | And you've come all the way from the pub like that, y'pillock!! |
| **JOHN:** | Listen everybody… |
| **SOUND:** | A countdown is heard, 6, 5, 4, 3… they all join in. |
| **JOHN:** | It's 1980, everyone. Happy New Year, everyone!! |
| **SOUND:** | Auld Lang Syne is heard and they all join in. The music continues through to the next scene. |
| **LIGHTING:** | Slow fade down. |

| | |
|---|---|
| **SLIDE 16:** | *"BSC AND THE UNIONS DIG IN FOR THE STRIKE."* <br> The Scotsman, 31st December. |
| **SLIDE 17:** | *"Pennies don't come from heaven, they have to be earned. No one would remember the Good Samaritan if he only had good intentions, he had money too."* <br> Margaret Thatcher, ITV Weekend World, <br> 7th January 1980. |
| **LIGHTING:** | Fade up. Early morning. External. |
| **SOUND:** | Slow fade off. |
| **ACT I Sc VI:** | **TONY, JEFF and MICK on picket duty.** <br> **A brazier is just about alight.** |
| **JEFF:** | How was y'festive season? |
| **TONY:** | Drunken and debauched! Met a nice tart New Year's Eve. |
| **JEFF:** | Did y'give her one? |
| **MICK:** | We had a traditional Christmas. I upset our lass, then the in-laws, and then fell asleep during the Sound of Music. |
| **TONY:** | Course I give her one, what d' y' think? |
| **JEFF:** | Well, y'don't exactly put it about, do y'? |

*JEFF tries to grab his genitals…*

| MICK: | Traditional prezzies too: cigarettes, socks and aftershave. The in-laws must think I'm a chain-smoking puff with sweaty feet. |
|---|---|
| TONY: | Read my Newsline if you're bored. |
| JEFF: | I'll stick to The Sun, thank you. I don't like all that claptrap propaganda. *(Beat)* We've drawn the short straw here, haven't we? |
| MICK: | Someone has to guard the back door, there'll always be one. |
| TONY: | Y'know they did a survey recently about newspapers. The Times is read by people who run the country, The Telegraph is read by people who think they run the country, The Guardian is read by people who would like to run the country. And the people who read /... |
| JEFF: | The Sun don't care who runs the country just as long as she's got big tits. *(He grabs hold of Tony)* Tell us summat we don't know. Listen citizen, you reckon y'gonna be part of some great and glorious revolution and y'still living with y'mam!! What's all that about, eh? Christ, when I was your age there wasn't a tart safe. |
| MICK: | And some things never change... |
| JEFF: | I'll tell y'Mick, this lot the Young Socialists hate Labour more than they do the Tories, aye! So come the Revolution, was all gonna be up against the wall. Why do we bother, eh? If it's not one extreme, it's another. |

TONY:              You don't know the first thing about politics…

JEFF:              Take it from me, comrade, you'll still be down
                   this shithole when y'65 cos you is playing
                   with y'self in more ways than one.

MICK:              Someone's coming, I knew it wouldn't be a waste.

JEFF:              He's mine. I'll get the bastard. *(Moves quickly)*

*Enter BRIAN WALLACE, he doesn't realise he's been spotted
as he sneaks forward.*

JEFF:              Morning, Squire. Don't y'know, there's a National
                   Strike on? *(Pause)* It's been in all the papers!!

*BRIAN sees JEFF and he tries to stand his ground, wondering whether
to go left or right. Then MICK and TONY join JEFF and they watch him
turn and go back.*

TONY:              Just what was he thinking?

MICK:              That's the trouble, he doesn't. No surprises.

LIGHTING:          Slow fade down.

**SLIDE 18:**     *"The BSC offer of 2% is now widely considered to have been a major public relations blunder."*
The Sunday Times, 13th January 1980.

**SLIDE 19:**     *"Now I've great sympathy for the steelworkers. But they have already had, and will continue to have, huge sums of money from the taxpayer, but by higher productivity."*
Sir Keith Joseph, Secretary of State for Industry, 17th January 1980.

**SLIDE 20:**     *Dear Sir Keith,*
*The logic is undoubtedly right. BUT!!*
*Miners 20%, Local Government 13%,*
*Civil Servants 14%.*
*Are these paid for by higher productivity?*
The Daily Mirror, 18th January 1980.

**LIGHTING:**     Fade up. General.

**ACT I Sc VII:**     **MR and MRS…**

**MR:**     We're getting by. You've gotta stick together in the bad times as well as the good. That's the promise you make when y'get married.

**MRS:**     Andy took an awful lot of persuading to sign the form… for Social Security… he doesn't like begging, you see.

**MR:**     If it wasn't for Dora's job in the shop we just wouldn't be able to cope, and with a little bit of Social Security… well, it all helps.

**MRS:**  Our three eldest daughters are all married to steel men so they are feeling the pinch more than us and with children of their own, they are not able to go to work.

**MR:**  Up to now… everything has been covered, mortgage and all the other usual bills.
We're planning a holiday in Scarborough…
last year we went to Majorca.

**MRS:**  We'll be lucky to make it to Scarborough, because our savings are just about gone. The thing is you see… we've never owed anyone, anything, ever in our lives before.

**LIGHTING:**  Slow fade down.

| LIGHTING: | Fade up. Internal. The Wilkinson's. Saturday morning. |
|---|---|

**ACT 1 Sc VIII:** **MAUREEN reads a newspaper; SUSAN has a play.**

| MAUR: | What's that y'reading, luv? |
|---|---|
| SUSAN: | 'The Crucible'. It's a play. |
| MAUR: | I know, by Arthur Miller? He was married to Marilyn Monroe. |
| SUSAN: | Think I've heard of her. |
| MAUR: | Y'dad used to fancy her. |
| SUSAN: | Mam!! |

*Enter JOHN drying his hair.*

| JOHN: | Oooh that's better. *(Beat)* Any chance of a cuppa, luv? |
|---|---|
| SUSAN: | I'll get it. |

*She exits. JOHN and MAUREEN share a surprised look.*

| JOHN: | Milk, no sugar. |
|---|---|
| SUSAN: | *(From the kitchen)* I have made it before, even if you can't remember! |
| MAUR: | How was it today then? |

**JOHN:** A few more than yesterday so the cracks improving. Funny how people react. Sometimes like "I really do think you have a valid claim, but I've got a family, a mortgage", they don't give a… Remember Charlie Mason, yeah? Turned up 9.30 this morning, nights last night, called out for a 6 till 2, and he'll be away by12.30.

**MAUR:** *(Surprised)* Charlie? Does that to his own mates?

**JOHN:** Exactly, sheer greed. A fella said, "I've just got me telephone bill" and someone shouted, "What's a telephone?'

*SUSAN brings in the drinks on a tray.*

**MAUR:** Biscuits as well? This could cost us, Dad.

**SUSAN:** Eee! Y'can't do anything in this house.
*(Sits with her book)*

**JOHN:** I stopped a bloke and he said I was the scum of the earth. So, I asked him what he thought of the Common Agricultural Policy. "What's that got to do with it?" he says. "A lot more than you think," I said.

**SUSAN:** Dad, why are you on strike?

**JOHN:** *(To Susan)* Because we think we've a valid claim, and we're not asking for a rise. *(Pause)* BSC say they will have to lay men off to pay us but I think the Government or rather Thatcher is controlling the situation. You have to make a stand. Yeah?

| | |
|---|---|
| **SUSAN:** | I think so… |
| **JOHN:** | How's the play coming on? |
| **SUSAN:** | I like the Courtroom scene. So dramatic. |
| **JOHN:** | Do you think Proctor is guilty? Sorry, I don't want to spoil it for you… he's made his confession, named his friends and he has to sign it. Even though he knows he will die, he says… "Leave me my name, you have taken my soul, please leave me my name" …great moment. Frances Nurse, didn't I, Mam? |
| **MAUR:** | Y'dad had so much talcum powder on to make him look old, he only had to move or touch his head and he gave off these 'clouds'. Looked like he was electing a new Pope!! |

*MAUREEN and SUSAN laugh at John's expense.*

| | |
|---|---|
| **SUSAN:** | I wish I had seen it… mind you, y'wouldn't need so much talc these days… would'y, Dad? |
| **JOHN:** | Watch it, young 'un. I can still put you over my knee. |

*This only causes more laughter.*

| | |
|---|---|
| **SOUND:** | Union City Blue – Blondie. |
| **LIGHTING:** | Fade down. |

| | |
|---|---|
| **SLIDE 21:** | *"HUMAN BARRICADES AT THE BSC"*<br>*Angry pickets' scuffle with the police.*<br>Evening Gazette, 28th January 1980. |
| **LIGHTING:** | Fade Up. |
| **SOUND:** | Fade off. |
| **ACT I Sc IX:** | **PICKET 2.** |
| **PICKET 2:** | There must have been about sixty of us, all screaming to be arrested. We'd been picketing this Steel Depot and we formed a barrier to stop lorries from bringing in supplies. Somehow, the Police had managed to get between us and this lorry and started chucking people out!! The bloody driver took this as a signal to come in and he just kept coming an' coming forward. We was all pushed backwards, squashed like. The next thing I knew, was a lad near me got lifted up in the air and dumped, no, impaled he was, on a fence. Someone said he was bleeding badly and had to be taken to hospital. Haven't heard how he is. *(Pause)* Then someone got arrested… for obstruction so we thought, fuck'em they'll have to arrest us all. When we got to the Police station, they said there was no need… they had got the man they wanted. *(Pause)* They've been given a free hand, you know? The Police. Is that what we want in this country? A Police State? They've got dogs, oh and they say they won't use them, but keep the van doors open, just so, you know they are there. So, you can hear them barking. Right? *(Pause)* The Government says it is fighting a war, and they've armed themselves with Parliament, |

the Courts, and now the Police with their dogs. And d'y'know what? We are fighting Marquis of Queensbury rules. It's not right, is it? *(Pause)* And whose side are you on? Eh?

LIGHTING:     Fade down.

| | |
|---|---|
| **LIGHTING:** | Fade up. Internal. The Wilkinson's. Tea time. |
| **ACT 1 Sc X:** | **JOHN is in the chair.**<br>**BILLY is at the table eating.**<br>**SUSAN enters.** |
| **JOHN:** | Did y'not hear y'Mother shout you? |
| **SUSAN:** | I'm not hungry, that's all. |
| **JOHN:** | Just not hungry? What? |
| **SUSAN:** | Had some toast, this morning. |
| **MAUR:** | Are y'not well, luv? |
| **SUSAN:** | No, I'm fine. Nowt's wrong. |
| **JOHN:** | I'll tell y'what's wrong, we could have saved that meal. |
| **MAUR:** | Try and be a bit more understanding, John. |
| **SUSAN:** | Why can't we have something else for a change? *(She pushes the plate away)* |
| **JOHN:** | *(He stands)* Be thankful we eat as well as we do under the circumstances. |

*SUSAN turns to go…*

| | |
|---|---|
| **JOHN:** | *(Angry)* Everyone is having to make do here…<br>I say we're doing alright. |

| SUSAN: | I just don't get it. Y'tell me to stick in at school, get good qualifications, keep my nose clean. British Steel is losing millions, there's too much steel in the world and you, you go on strike! |
|---|---|
| JOHN: | Susan, they're two separate issues. |
| SUSAN: | *(She won't back down)* You said, if we are to get to America, we would have to make savings, right? So, if British Steel needs to make savings? Well? |
| JOHN: | There's more at stake than a trip to Disneyland. There's 50,000 jobs gone already, where do you think it's all gonna end eh? Well, you can forget all about America, do you hear me? And you can start doing as y'bloody told right?! |
| SUSAN: | *(Moves closer)* Haven't you always prided yourself in not being a yes-man? |

*It is all too much for JOHN, he lashes out…*

| MAUR: | John no!! |

*SUSAN runs out screaming, followed by MAUREEN.*
*BILLY gets up to join them.*

| JOHN: | Where do you think you're going? |
| BILLY: | I'm finished… please can I leave the table? |
| JOHN: | And take your plate with you. |

*BILLY goes out and MAUREEN returns. Prolonged silence.*

**JOHN:** I will not be spoken to like that… and in my own home.

**MAUR:** She's only a child, John, she's trying to understand.

*MAUREEN waits for JOHN to say something, but he doesn't. She exits.*

**LIGHTING:** Fade down.

| | |
|---|---|
| **SLIDE 22:** | *"When you remember this Gov's attitude to Communist bloc countries, well here we have imported Coil Steel from East Germany, to make cars and washing machines. Thatcher would rather import Communist steel, than pay her own workers a living wage."* Scunthorpe Striker, ITV World In Action, 4th February 1980. |
| **SLIDE 23:** | *"BSC failed to reach a deal with craftsmen as a delegate conference rejected a 14% offer with a 2:1 majority."* The Guardian, 15th February 1980. |
| **LIGHTING:** | Fade up. Internal. General. |
| **ACT I Sc XI:** | **A WORKER'S STORY.** |
| **WORKER:** | I've been at British Steel now for 15 years and a fully paid up member of the ISTC. The Iron and Steel Trades Confederation, no less. *(Pause)* Because I'm single I can't claim anything. I've been to the Union three times and the Social Security twice and no one will give me any money. What if I do live on my own? I'm still running up debt. I pay my rent, but I've run out of food…*(Angry)* Y'don't get the top brass or the full time officials down here, you've only got your mates on the picket line. They've got television crews and everything in London. They are not interested in us who pay their wages. *(Pause)* Bill Sirs might be able to give up what he gets but the likes of us can't afford it. I don't think he's got the 100% support he says he's got and a ballot would prove it. How about it, Sirs? |
| **LIGHTING:** | Fade down. |

| | |
|---|---|
| **LIGHTING:** | Fade up. Internal. The Wilkinson's. Afternoon. |
| **ACT I Sc XII:** | **MAUREEN, SHEILA and WENDY are having a cuppa and a catch up.** |
| **WENDY:** | Well, I think it's not right, for a mother to work and leave her children. |
| **SHEILA:** | Yeah, I used to think that but then money rears its ugly head. Again and again. |
| **WENDY:** | You already have a full time job with your husband, family, and your home. Why take on a cleaning job? |
| **SHEILA:** | Y'learn quick, Wendy. And any of my lot that mess the house and don't clean up, they'll be found in a jar on top of Eston Hills. |
| **MAUR:** | Ooh I'll say. Got to be mean, to keep them keen, 'avent'y? More tea, anyone? |

*MAUREEN and SHEILA try not to laugh.*

| | |
|---|---|
| **WENDY:** | But children need a mother's time, a mother's love… |
| **SHEILA:** | But for how long? They grow and soon they need fish fingers, spaghetti hoops, clothes that don't last five minutes, and a room of their own. Imagine what would happen if I tried to read them… a s-t-o-r-y? |
| **MAUR:** | They'd be phoning the men in white coats, for sure. |

**SHEILA:** Somebody has to clean the toilets, haven't they, Maureen? Did you know that 5% of people on Teesside work at ICI? The other 95% just sit and watch 'em.

*MAUREEN and SHEILA laugh.*

**WENDY:** Ooh, and I certainly couldn't go in a men's toilet.

**SHEILA:** The women are just as bad. Why can't women park cars? *(She holds up a hand with a small gap between her thumb and forefinger)* Because men keep telling us that's seven and a half inches. D'y'get it?

*SHEILA and MAUREEN continue to laugh,*
*WENDY covers her unease by producing a catalogue.*

**WENDY:** I thought I'd show just a couple of things I've already bought. Lovely porcelain figures. Look at the detail on the face and in the hair.

*MAUREEN and SHEILA exchange looks.*

**WENDY:** Real quality for 4.99. Actually, this figure comes in a set of four, just the thing for your china cabinet.

**SHEILA:** What china cabinet?

**WENDY:** *(Struggling)* Well let me show you the wine glasses on page 17. All made by traditional British craftsmen, just the thing for a drop of Blue Nun, a subtle blend of extravagance and excellence.

| | |
|---|---|
| **MAUR:** | Blue Nun? |
| **SHEILA:** | Brian won't have it in the house…<br>Barley Wine more like. |

WENDY *tries to maintain her composure.*

| | |
|---|---|
| **WENDY:** | Look… I'll leave the catalogue and you'll find the party plan at the back. I could get a crowd together, no pressure to buy. And… there is a lovely little present for the hostess. |
| **MAUR:** | I'm sure it would be a laugh, Wendy, not at the moment, thanks. |
| **SHEILA:** | A hostess dressed as a Blue Nun, now I can see Brian going for that. *(She laughs)* Ee, is that the time? *(She moves to go)* Nearly forgot, Maur, they sometimes need extra staff at our place, would y'be interested? |
| **MAUR:** | The money would be helpful. Er I'll have a word with John. Things are a bit, y'know? But, I'll let you know. Thanks. |
| **SHEILA:** | Just thought I'd mention it… I'll see me'self out. Bye. |
| **MAUR:** | Bye Sheila. |
| **WENDY:** | Bye. |

*Silence.*

**WENDY:**     The strains are starting to tell? Picketing all day now, is he?

**MAUR:**     Probably gone for a game of snooker with the lads.

**WENDY:**     Nearly two months on strike and you let him go boozing!

**MAUR:**     He drinks orange. And I know what y'getting at, I was listening.

*MAUREEN starts to clear up.*

**WENDY:**     Working women.

**MAUR:**     Women have always worked, supported their families, in wartime and peacetime. *(Pause)* Isn't your party plan work? Well?

**WENDY:**     What if I did have a baby and went back to work? Would Peter get involved? I don't want much out of life. A nice home, a family and a husband that goes to work every day.

**MAUR:**     Well two out of three ain't bad. *(Pause)* Pete still firing blanks, is he?

*JOHN is heard offstage "Honey I'm home" and after more noises, he stumbles in with a sausage dangling from his open flies. WENDY screams at what she thinks she sees and hurries out.*

**JOHN:**     *(Shouts)* It's alright, Wend, won 2nd prize in the Meat Draw.

**MAUR:**     What the bloody hell y'playing at?

**JOHN:**        They're Newboulds!!

*MAUREEN gets her coat.*

**JOHN:**        Where'y going? With the kids at…
a thought we could…y'know?

*JOHN goes to kiss her and MAUREEN pushes him away.*

**MAUR:**        You'll be needing bloody Newboulds by the time
I'm finished with y'.

**JOHN:**        Can't we have a laugh anymore, eh?
An' where y'going?

*Maureen goes to get her coat and puts it on.*

**MAUR:**        Get something edible for tea. *(She smells beer)*
You've been drinking haven't'y'?

*JOHN is stopped in his tracks.*

**MAUR:**        Havent'y?!!

*MAUREEN wait buts gets no answer.*

**MAUR:**        Christ, that's all I need.

*She exits in disgust. JOHN knows he's crossed a line.*

**SOUND:**        Cavatina – John Williams.

**LIGHTING:**        Slow fade down.

### INTERVAL.

# ACT II

LIGHTING:     Fade up.

ACT II Sc I:     **ANGRY RATEPAYER, 50s.**

R'PAYER:     The Councillors, who are supporting the
striking steel workers with rent and rate rebates.
Is this support based on hypocrisy, ignorance
or both? Workers in profitable industries can
demand and even deserve large increases.
The unprofitable ones get smaller rises or none
at all. Do Councillors realise that everyone in
this land are contributing to British Steel?

As a Public Service worker who has been offered
7%, is there really one law for manufacturing and
another for Public and Health Services, where
striking is considered a disgraceful disruption of
public welfare. *(Pause)* I suggest the Steel unions
run a secret ballot and discover just how keen
their members really are for striking.

LIGHTING:     Fade down.

| | |
|---|---|
| **SLIDE 24:** | *POWER WORKERS 19% DEAL. Yesterday, Electricians' leader Frank Chapple, won the rise after two hours of talks.*<br>The Sun, 7th March 1980. |
| **SLIDE 25:** | *BALLOT ON BALLOT: BOTH SIDES CLAIM VICTORY.*<br>The Guardian, 10th March 1980. |
| **SLIDE 26:** | *STATE BOSSES TO RECEIVE £400 A WEEK RISE.*<br>The Sun, 30th March 1980. |
| **LIGHTING:** | Fade up. Internal. The Wilkinson's. Sunday morning. |
| **ACT II Sc II:** | **JOHN is in the chair, reading the paper.** |

*SUSAN enters, sees JOHN, goes to leave.*

**JOHN:**      Hello, luv…

**SUSAN:**      Have y'seen Mam?

**JOHN:**      Round Nana's. Can I help?

**SUSAN:**      Erm… I just needed to ask her something.

**JOHN:**      Is it about Stratford?

**SUSAN:**      Er… yeah.

*Silence.*

| | |
|---|---|
| **SUSAN:** | What? Can't afford it, right!? I never go anywhere me… just like America. It's part of my O Levels, I have to go!! |
| **JOHN:** | If I could finish… please. *(JOHN searches his pockets and produces a crumpled fiver)* Will that do to be going on with? |
| **SUSAN:** | Thanks. |

*She goes to leave.*

| | |
|---|---|
| **JOHN:** | We've hardly spoken since… |
| **SUSAN:** | Since you lashed out at me? *(Pause)* Y'can't say it, can y'? |
| **JOHN:** | That's because I can't believe I did it. |
| **SUSAN:** | Well, you did. |
| **JOHN:** | I've done some stupid things in my time, as Mam will tell y'. But there's no excuse for what I did. I'm not proud of it, either. |
| **SUSAN:** | Us kids are also under pressure, what with school and exams. *(Pause)* Some friends know what you do and I've been called names a couple of times. |
| **JOHN:** | Friends? Have you told your teacher? |
| **SUSAN:** | No, Dad, it will make it worse. |
| **JOHN:** | I can come up to school and sort it out? |

**SUSAN:** No, you're doing it again, Dad. I know you're doing something for a reason, even if they don't or don't want to. Their loss. *(Pause)* This is about you.

*Silence.*

**JOHN:** Yes of course… I shouldn't have lost it; I just shouldn't have. I am so sorry.

*Silence. JOHN opens his arms offering a cuddle.*
*SUSAN resists and offers her hand.*

**SUSAN:** I accept your apology. Y'can't blame me for being angry about America.

**JOHN:** No, luv, of course not.

*JOHN goes to give SUSAN a hug and she holds out her hand.*
*Silence. They shake on it.*

**JOHN:** We'd better make sure you get to Stratford then!!

**SUSAN:** Thanks, Dad.

*Both seem grateful for the moment.*

**LIGHTING:** Fade down.

| | |
|---|---|
| **LIGHTING:** | Fade up. External. General. |
| **ACT II Sc III:** | **BATTLING HOUSEWIFE.** |
| **H'WIFE:** | I think the strike has dragged on too long, they talk on and on, but are getting nowhere…we've lost our pride, our husbands' wages, some have lost much more. I spoke to some thirty women, who all wanted to mount a demonstration and I'm sure there would be a lot more. *(Pause)* |
| | There were just eight of us when we marched from the Gazette to the ISTC Union, I would have marched on my own if I had to. I wanted to make a point. They had the Strikers' Reception Committee waiting for us, it was pathetic. Outnumbering us 7:1. You should have heard them, "Why don't you go home and get your old man's tea ready?" I replied, "What with?" We're not against the strike, we are against what the strike has become. We want the Union to pull out middle management, stop all safety cover, because that will put an end to the strike. All this publicity in the press? I think we have been misunderstood. I'm not very good with words, y'see. We're not saying the men should go back now, whatever the cost. Let's face it, the men can't back down now. *(Pause)* |
| | My husband doesn't agree with the offer and with a lot of what I say. But that doesn't mean he will stop me expressing my opinions unlike some I could mention. We're just pawns in a political battle, we're not trying to be political heroines… all we wanted was to put our point of view. |
| **LIGHTING:** | Fade down. |

| | |
|---|---|
| **SLIDE 27:** | *"LOSERS ALL ROUND."*<br>*Just one $^1/2\%$ more… after all these weeks.*<br>Daily Express, 1st April 1980. |
| **SLIDE 28:** | *"TRAGEDY OF A PROUD STRIKER."*<br>*Pride prevented a BSC office worker from*<br>*accepting financial help from her family,*<br>*and they took an overdose.*<br>Daily Mirror, 2nd April 1980. |
| **SLIDE 29:** | *"I was quite excited at the prospect of taking on*<br>*the problems at British Steel. In a way I was doing*<br>*something important for the country."*<br>Ian McGregor on his appointment, May 1980. |
| **LIGHTING:** | Fade Up. Internal. |
| **ACT II Sc IV:** | **Engineer DICK meets JOHN in the**<br>**Locker Room.** |
| **DICK:** | What's with the Oven Top gauges? Arthur says y'haven't started yet? |
| **JOHN:** | That's right. Cos of the fumes. |
| **DICK:** | You've had all morning, surely y'did one or two? |
| **JOHN:** | If y'don't believe me, ask the production lads. |
| **DICK:** | I'm asking you. Have you tried the oxygen line? |
| **JOHN:** | Most of the lads won't use it, too much condensation. |
| **DICK:** | So y'just gonna… sit round all day and do nowt? |

| | |
|---|---|
| **JOHN:** | Just because the strike is over, doesn't mean we have to put ourselves at risk, does it? Get one of your contractors to do it. |
| **DICK:** | I'd get more sense out of them. |
| **JOHN:** | They've been taken on to do jobs we would normally do? |
| **DICK:** | You're doing nowt anyways. |
| **JOHN:** | They've stopped the overtime. We can't pay our debts. Talk about rubbing our noses in it. |
| **DICK:** | Look, y'not Shop Steward now, y'know! |
| **JOHN:** | A paycut or lose jobs? Catch 22 or what? |
| **DICK:** | Trust you to get all political. I hear you're after redundancy? |
| **JOHN:** | How long were you shop steward? Long enough to get y'feet under the table. |
| **DICK:** | So, it's true? Some of us can't afford it. |
| **JOHN:** | If Consett and Corby are anything to go by, we won't have any fucking choice, will we? |
| **DICK:** | What's a good union man doing taking 'blood money'? |
| **JOHN:** | Don't you 'blood money' me… whichever way you look at it, targets, health and safety, pensions, it's all blood money. And, it's keeping you in a job. |

**DICK:**        Are y'gonna to do owt or what?

**JOHN:**        As soon as it's safe up there. I'll keep y'posted, shall I?

*JOHN exits.*

**DICK:**        *(Fuming)* Fucking troublemaker. Keep that up an' you won't be leaving with a fat cheque in your back pocket.

**SOUND:**       Stop the Cavalry – Jona Lewie.

**LIGHTING:**    Fade down.

| | |
|---|---|
| **SLIDE 30:** | *"I couldn't live without work. That's what makes me so sympathetic to these people who are unemployed. I don't know how they live without work."* Mrs Thatcher, News Of The World, 4th May 1980. |
| **SLIDE 31:** | *BSC Chairman, Ian MacGregor, postpones the annual rise for six months. Tomorrow, he plans to announce the further closures of 20,000 jobs.* The Sunday Times, 14th December 1980. |
| **SLIDE 32** | March 1981. |
| **LIGHTING:** | Fade up. Internal. The Wilkinson's Lounge. |
| **SOUND:** | Fade off. |
| **ACT II Sc V:** | **Saturday morning, JOHN reads the paper. MAUREEN appears at the door and watches him for a while, then enters.** |
| **MAUR:** | I like it when y'weekend off, we get a bit of time to us 'selves. |
| **JOHN:** | This sounds like work or… be gentle with me… Maur. |
| **MAUR:** | What are you talking about? |
| **JOHN:** | So, it's a list of jobs longer than y'mothers face? |
| **MAUR:** | Do you mind!! She's been very good to us. *(Beat)* Any post this morning? |
| **JOHN:** | Just the one. |

*He uncovers an official looking brown envelope and passes it to her.*

JOHN: Here, read it yourself…

MAUR: What's the mystery, have we come into money?

JOHN: Y'could say that.

*She reads.*

MAUR: John!!

JOHN: I was going to say something.

MAUR: When?

JOHN: I knew y'would be worried!!

MAUR: Worried?!! What was the strike for, John?

JOHN: I put in for redundancy… I wanted to take us to America. I wanted to make it up to the kids, they were so disappointed.

MAUR: An y'thought… the strike's over, no overtime. Where can I get a few bob from? I know. I'll take redundancy.

JOHN: It's not that simple. I knew you wouldn't understand.

MAUR: Well, if you don't tell me things, how can I? *(Beat)* Don't forget we still owe my mother or are y'planning to take her to America as well?

| | |
|---|---|
| **JOHN:** | *(Under his breath)* No, they've got their own Mafia there. |
| **MAUR:** | What did you say? |
| **JOHN:** | It's a chance to make a new start!! |
| **MAUR:** | Doing what, may I ask? |
| **JOHN:** | Y'forever saying y'right behind me. But when it comes to it, as long as I do what you want, you're fine. I've had enough. |

*JOHN exits.*

| | |
|---|---|
| **MAUR:** | *(Calls)* Is that it, John? We're supposed to be a family. It's what couples do, a bit of give and take. |

*She sits down and talks to herself.*

| | |
|---|---|
| **MAUR:** | I suppose I ought to be thankful that you didn't lash out at me. *(Pause)* In all this time, you've never said a word and now, guess what? It's my fault. |

*She gets upset. BILLY enters.*

| | |
|---|---|
| **BILLY:** | Mam, Mam, are you alright? |
| **MAUR:** | I'm okay, Billy. *(She tries to recover)* |
| **BILLY:** | Is it Grandad? Were y'thinking about Grandad? |

*He cuddles her.*

| | |
|---|---|
| **MAUR:** | Aye, I was thinking about Grandad. |

*Silence.*

*JOHN returns with 'damage limitation' on his mind.*

| | |
|---|---|
| **JOHN:** | Look I'm sorry / I should have… |
| **MAUR:** | *(Beat)* Sheila says there could be a job for me if I'm interested. |
| **JOHN:** | Doing what? Eh? I'm not having you work as a cleaner |
| **BILLY:** | When's dinner ready, Mam? |
| **MAUR:** | Soon, love. |
| **BILLY:** | But I'm hungry now. |
| **JOHN:** | Sheila's putting ideas into y'head, is she? |
| **MAUR:** | She's a very good friend. I am allowed to have friends, aren't I? |
| **JOHN:** | No wife / of mine… |
| **MAUR:** | And Sheila is totally disgusted at Brian if you bothered / to ask her!! |
| **JOHN:** | Is working as a cleaner, you're a secretary. |
| **MAUR:** | I was a typist. Nobody is offering me work as a typist!! |

*BILLY interrupts.*

**BILLY:**    Can I have some crisps?

**JOHN:**    Billy, go to your room.

**BILLY:**    You go to your room, you're the one that's
upsetting everyone.

**JOHN:**    *(He turns on him)* I'll smack you so hard,
you won't sit down for a week.

**MAUR:**    Go to your room, Billy, please.

*BILLY looks at MAUREEN and then exits.*

**JOHN:**    That's another thing /

**MAUR:**    Have a go at me, by all means.
First Susan, now Billy. Who's next, John?

*Silence.*

**JOHN:**    He's getting too big for his boots.

**MAUR:**    And what about you? You're drinking nearly
every day. Betting shops? Y'never used to gamble.
And... you took redundancy so we could still go
to America. Yeah? That's all gone by the board
now, hasn't it? Well?

**JOHN:**    That's nothing to do with you getting a job as a
cleaner.

**MAUR:**    Says who? *(Pause)* Be careful what you say next...

*Silence.*

**MAUR:** I've got news for you. I'm going to take this job because we need the money and if you don't like it... then call me scab, if that makes you feel better!!

*MAUREEN waits for a reaction. There isn't one. She exits.*

*BILLY enters.*

**BILLY:** Can y'fix me bike, Dad?

**JOHN:** Yeah sure... this afternoon.

*JOHN picks up the paper.*

**BILLY:** But I want to go out now...

**JOHN:** Y'dinner's gonna be ready soon. *(Beat)* Played any school football recently?

**BILLY:** Yes. But you never normally ask. I think it's a slow puncture.

**JOHN:** Nothing serious then! *(He continues to read)*

**BILLY:** Dad? Do you still love Mam?

**JOHN:** *(JOHN stops reading)* Of course, Billy. Why?

**BILLY:** Why? She is always crying. Something else you haven't noticed?

**JOHN:** Why all these questions, Billy?

**BILLY:** I just want to know.

**JOHN:** You remember when we were all on strike and...

**BILLY:** And we didn't go to America!

**JOHN:** Yes, we got into debt and even though we had savings... and y'Mam being such a good mother, worried too much...

**BILLY:** So, why haven't you got a job now, Dad?

**JOHN:** So many jobs lost, less money being spent in the shops, in the community. They didn't know it would affect everyone.

**BILLY:** Did you know?

**JOHN:** I had an idea, yeah.

**BILLY:** Then why did y'give up y'job?

**JOHN:** Because, because... if I hadn't, they would have just ridden roughshod over the lot of us, Billy!! I just tried to look after my fellow workers, but what a waste of time.

*Silence.*

**BILLY:** If you had worked, Dad, we could have gone to America!!

**JOHN:**     God, Billy, I know you are trying to understand,
         but if you ever turn out like one of those…
         I'll swing for you, Billy; do you hear me?
         *(He grabs Billy)* Billy, do you hear me?

**BILLY:**     Dad, Dad, y'hurting me!

*JOHN realises and releases BILLY, who goes out.*

**V.O:**     Are y'coming Dad? Mam said y'would!

*JOHN stares into space.*

**LIGHTING:**     Slow fade down.

| | |
|---|---|
| **SLIDE 33:** | *"Llanwern continues to produce 2 million tonnes, with less than half its workforce."* The Guardian, 14th May 1982. |
| **LIGHTING:** | Fade up. Internal. The Club. |
| **ACT II SC VI:** | **Sunday afternoon at the Club. BRIAN and PETER swap stories.** |
| **BRIAN:** | So, I said to our lass… "How come you don't moan and groan when we're making love, like?" |
| **PETER:** | An' what did she say? |
| **BRIAN:** | She seemed all for it, so there I was banging away, an then our lass says "Are you ever gonna finish that bloody bathroom or what?!" *(They both laugh)* |
| **PETER:** | Wendy's not speaking to me… |
| **BRIAN:** | Why not like? |
| **PETER:** | She wants to go to Greece next year and I've said no. What's wrong with Majorca all of a sudden? |
| **BRIAN:** | Think this year, me an' our lass will be in Loggerheads, again. |
| **PETER:** | It's in Scotland, isn't it? *(They both laugh)* |

*MICK appears with a round of drinks*

| | |
|---|---|
| **MICK:** | Sorry lads, after the Bingo, y'got more chance of getting a pint off Lord Lucan. |

*JOHN returns from the loo.*

**JOHN:** Lord Lucan, I didn't know he was a member? *(Beat)* Eh, I've heard they are starting men on the complex, Davies Engineering.

**PETER:** I thought you took redundancy for a career in academia?

**BRIAN:** I bet he can't even spell it... go on, spell it... a... k...

**JOHN:** Not now, Dumbo...

**BRIAN:** We all remember you when you had nowt.

**MIKE:** Brian, stop!

**BRIAN:** Fat lot of good, the strike was. How much was it? Half a percent more? *(Beat)* You going to college? YTS in Flower Arranging more like.

**JOHN:** *(He turns)* I'll rearrange your face, y'daft get. You didn't even go on strike... did y'? Eh? It cost you nothing. Not a penny.

*MICK tries to intervene.*

**MICK:** Come on lads, everyone's laughing at y', bloody give over.

**JOHN:** *(To Brian)* So don't come shouting the odds or I'll punch y'fucking lights out!

*JOHN is still holding BRIAN. The bell goes for last orders.*

**BRIAN:**          Aye well, no point in missing last orders, eh?
                    I'll get them.

*JOHN finally lets go of BRIAN. Puts his hand in his pocket and chucks money on the table.*

**JOHN:**           Don't even go there, scab... my shout.

*JOHN goes to leave.*

**PETER:**          Leaving before chucking out time? On a Sunday?
                    Your lass must have you right under the thumb,
                    eh Brian?

**JOHN:**           And what would you two, know about things like
                    that, eh?

*JOHN stares at PETER then exits. BRIAN picks up the money, says nothing and goes to the bar.*

**LIGHTING:**       Fade down.

| | |
|---|---|
| **LIGHTING:** | Fade up. Internal. The Wilkinson's. A little later. |
| **ACT II Sc VII:** | **SUSAN is putting on makeup, BILLY is on the settee, while MAUREEN irons.** |
| **BILLY:** | Are we going to our Nan's, or what? |
| **MAUR:** | Yes, we are… I'll just finish this. |
| **SUSAN:** | I thought Dad was coming… |
| **BILLY:** | I'm hungry now… |
| **SUSAN:** | You always are. Eyes / bigger than… |
| **BILLY:** | Not as big as your gob. Sure y'got enough lipstick? |
| **MAUR:** | Look, if y'both ready, why not go on ahead, and take the flowers. They're in the sink. |

*BILLY is up like a shot.*

| | |
|---|---|
| **BILLY:** | They're in the sink, Sis. Your turn. Loser. |

*SUSAN, world weary teenager, mopes out. MAUREEN breathes a sigh of relief, then continues to iron her blouse. Silence.*

*JOHN enters with a bottle of sherry.*

| | |
|---|---|
| **MAUR:** | Blimey, did they run out of beer or didn't y'win the Meat Draw? |
| **JOHN:** | I said I wouldn't be late, remember? |

*MAUREEN finishes the ironing and takes it out. Silence.*

**JOHN:**  *(Shouting)* I've been talking to one of the lads.
There's a chance of a few months' work with
Davies Engineering on the complex.

*Silence. MAUREEN returns with her blouse on.*

**JOHN:**  I'll go down tomorrow first thing.

**MAUR:**  Those the contractors y'were calling scabs?

**JOHN:**  If you can work as a cleaner,
I can do that for sure.

**MAUR:**  Given up on your college idea?

**JOHN:**  I can do both, can't I?

*Pause.*

**MAUR:**  Are you asking me or telling me?

**JOHN:**  I'm… asking you.

*MAUREEN points to the sherry.*

**MAUR:**  That for me?

**JOHN:**  Sherry? Since when? It's for your Mother!

**MAUR:**  Sucking up to the Mafia now, are'y'?

**JOHN:**  *(John gives her a look)*
She is cooking us Sunday lunch.

**MAUR:** I'm surprised y'didn't put it down y'trousers and pretend to be The Count of Monte Christo! *(She laughs) (Beat)* It's never bothered you before, has it?

**JOHN:** What's that supposed to mean?

*Silence.*

**JOHN:** Well?

**MAUR:** It would appear, you're appealing to me, through me Mam?

**JOHN:** Would you rather I went back to the Club?

*Silence.*

**JOHN:** I'm not a mind reader.

**MAUR:** Neither am I? Your redundancy plans, for example?

**JOHN:** Not again, Maureen?

**MAUR:** Still don't get it, do you?

**JOHN:** I have already apologised. And I do so again.

*Silence.*

**JOHN:** I thought we were going to your Mam's?

MAUR:          And you've bought a bottle of cheap sherry.
               'Cos that's a man's job apparently. Hunter,
               gatherer and provider. Is that right, John?
               Have I missed anything?

JOHN:          She is expecting us.

MAUR:          And all I had to do was cook, sew and clean for
               you and the kids. Remember them?

*Silence. MAUREEN goes out and returns with her coat, and puts it on.*

JOHN:          Maureen, I know you don't believe me.

MAUR:          Let me finish, John! You see when I took the
               cleaning job, I wasn't attacking you, John,
               I was trying to feed my family, that's all it was.
               That's all it ever was. Looking after my family.
               Right? Just like you.

*Silence.*

JOHN:          I realise now, I shouldn't have taken it out on…
               you and the kids.

MAUR:          God, you were just so… angry… all the time.
               I've never seen you…

JOHN:          I know, I brought it all home. Every bit of it.

*JOHN stands like a little boy lost…*

JOHN:          So, is that it then?

*Silence.*

**MAUR:**     Think… I'm gonna kick you out?

*Silence.*

**MAUR:**     Oh, I'm not letting you off the hook that easily.

**JOHN:**     Woo!! What'y'talkin about?

**MAUR:**     Listen to me now. You get some contract work, till college starts. It'll keep you out of my way, if nothing else.

*Pause.*

**MAUR:**     Thinking of getting a proper office job, rather than just cleaning it.

**JOHN:**     With 21 hours study a week, I can still claim. A Tory councillor told me.

**MAUR:**     And you believed him? Well, you're gonna have to trust me.

**JOHN:**     Trust you? What you talking about? Is that a yes then?

**MAUR:**     Did you tell them about your spelling?

**JOHN:**     I won't, if you won't? *(Beat)* Are we going to your Mother's?

*Silence.*

**JOHN:**     It would be a shame to waste a cheap bottle of British sherry.

**MAUR:**          If you weren't so much like…

*They stare at each other for a while and JOHN tentatively opens his arms for a hug. Silence. MAUREEN returns the embrace. They get their things and exit.*

**LIGHTING:**     Fade down.

| | |
|---|---|
| **SLIDE 34:** | *"My father worked in steel, and the years I've worked here I've enjoyed my job. But there's nothing else to do round here. But my son is on the dole and we can't employ any new men... it's heart-breaking."* Plant Manager, Port Talbot, South Wales. |
| **SLIDE 35:** | *"Unemployment reaches 2,680,977 (11.8% of the workforce), Margaret Thatcher is warned that a further rise is likely."* UK Government report, New York Times, July 22 1981. |
| **LIGHTING:** | Fade up. Internal. The Pub. Mid-evening. |
| **ACTII Sc VIII:** | **WENDY and PETER, BRIAN AND SHEILA in the pub, women on one side, men on the other.** |
| **WENDY:** | So, you've not had our card yet? |
| **SHEILA:** | No. They usually arrive after y'get back, don't the'? Where was it you said you went? |
| **WENDY:** | Pefkos in Rhodes. It's a Greek Island. |
| **BRIAN:** | Pefkos? Sounds like a trade union. I thought you said you were going Majorca again, Pete? |
| **PETER:** | Fancied a change. Travel agent said everyone will be going soon. |
| **BRIAN:** | I don't think we will. Sheila doesn't travel well, y'see. |

*Sheila glares at Brian.*

**SHEILA:** Bit rich, coming from someone who refers to anything that isn't English food, as... foreign muck!!

**WENDY:** You should give it a try, Sheila... they all speak English!

**SHEILA:** Was it a hotel you stayed in?

**WENDY:** No, an apartment, self-catering.

**SHEILA:** Self-catering? And that's your idea of a holiday?

**BRIAN:** Couldn't afford a hotel then, Pete? *(Beat)* Gonna show us y'white bits then, Wend!!

**SHEILA:** *(Whispering)* Will you give over!

**WENDY:** Oh, look, John and Maureen, give them a wave!

*JOHN and MAUREEN arrive with their drinks, hellos are exchanged. WENDY gestures to MAUREEN, but she chooses to stay next to JOHN.*

**PETER:** What time do you call this? I'll get these.

**BRIAN:** I know, John, just like you said... got Maureen right where she wants y!

**MAUR:** Thanks for the card, Wendy. Did you have a nice time?

**WENDY:** Lovely thanks, not too crowded.

**BRIAN:** *(Whispering)* I bet she didn't even send us one!

| | |
|---|---|
| **SHEILA:** | Ever wonder why, Brian? Calm down and try not to show me up again. |
| **JOHN:** | Right then, a little announcement. |
| **BRIAN:** | Elvis is dead! *(No one laughs except Brian)* |

*SHEILA glares at him.*

| | |
|---|---|
| **JOHN:** | I've been accepted at Kirby College. |
| **BRIAN:** | As an odd job man? |
| **SHEILA:** | Brian!! |

*PETER returns with a tray of drinks.*

| | |
|---|---|
| **JOHN:** | O and A levels, actually. |
| **BRIAN:** | Doing what? |
| **JOHN:** | Midwifery, Chartered Accountancy, keeping our options open, eh Maureen? |

*They exchange looks.*

| | |
|---|---|
| **SHEILA:** | Congratulations, John. But how will you manage? |
| **MAUR:** | Well, there's still some of John's redundancy  money… |
| **JOHN:** | You also get Re-adaption Benefit to retrain. Change jobs even. |
| **WENDY:** | But what else can you do? Even with retraining? |

**JOHN:**    I don't know, Wendy, but I think we are going to find out, aren't we, Maureen?

*They share a smile.*

**WENDY:**    Peter's worked hard and ICI have been good to him, what with shares and everything.

**JOHN:**    The recession isn't just British Steel, it's worldwide, just ask your mate, Thatcher.

**BRIAN:**    I wish somebody would give me a year's wages to retrain.

**SHEILA:**    Brian, you didn't even go on strike, did y'?

*Silence.*

**PETER:**    So, if this recession is worldwide, we need to be more efficient, increase production. It's not political, right.

**JOHN:**    Heard about the BSC's ten year plan, that focused on five main steel areas, including Redcar, to produce 35mn tonnes of steel. A recession kicks in, we don't need 35 million tonnes, we only need 15 million tonnes. The bosses cock up and the workers branded lazy.

**WENDY:**    But the unions have too much power, haven't they?

**PETER:**    And Mrs Thatcher is doing something about it.

JOHN: The unions were not responsible for the restructuring of BSC. Are you in a union, Peter?

PETER: Er, we have Workers Councils, with negotiations between the management and the men, but some are union members.

JOHN: MacGregor wasn't there to negotiate, he'll pay off another 20,000, if they don't like it, he'll close the bloody lot down. *(Pause.)*

WENDY: Thatcher is doing her best for the country, can't you see that?

JOHN: Thatcher always blames the workers,
so companies can close down factories
and open up in Rumania or Venezuela.
They are also exporting cash, aren't they?
If the unions have got too much power,
how come they can't stop that happening?

WENDY: They have to look after the shareholders.

JOHN: But they aren't the wealth creators, are they?

BRIAN: Some unions try to bring down the Government.

SHEILA: Shouldn't governments be accountable?
I think they should.

PETER: Ted Heath lost an election because of the miners.

JOHN:          Heath called the election, not the miners and he
               lost it. Then lost control of the Conservatives,
               let in Thatcher and the rest is history. You could
               say the unions helped put Thatcher where she is
               today. And not a word of thanks!!

PETER:         Where do you get all this stuff from?

JOHN:          I read... there isn't a law against that as well,
               is there?

BRIAN:         Sounds... subversive, if you ask me.

JOHN:          They thought the Tolpuddle Martyrs were
               subversive and transported them. The problem
               for the unions all along, is they took the masses
               out of the gutter, but didn't get the chance to
               educate them. *(To Brian)* You're in the union,
               but didn't strike. That's your democratic right.
               *(Pause)* But democracy doesn't just happen on
               Election Day, does it? *(Silence. JOHN's had
               enough)* Sup up, Maureen, we're going.

*MAUREEN and JOHN finish their drinks and move towards the door.
JOHN turns to speak.*

JOHN:          You know, a Conservative isn't someone
               who just uses the missionary position.

*SHEILA laughs.*

MAUR:          Sheila, if I don't see y'at work,
               I'll pop round next week, okay?

*JOHN and MAUREEN exit. Silence*

**BRIAN:** Y'know, I knew him when he was just an electrician.

**WENDY:** I've always thought there was something stuck up about those two, sort of snobbish. Especially, Maureen. Do you need the loo, Sheila?

*SHEILA pretends she hasn't heard.*

**WENDY:** Well, I do!!

*WENDY reaches for her bag and waits. SHEILA can no longer refuse and gets up.*

**SHEILA:** I need another drink, Brian, make it a double. And some cashews.

*As they go, WENDY is heard to say...*

**WENDY:** Sheila, did I ever tell you about the time when John came home drunk?

*After they have gone...*

**BRIAN:** What's the missionary position?

**PETER:** Don't ask me, I didn't vote for Thatcher.

**BRIAN:** Same again, then?

**PETER:** Aye.

*Brian goes to the bar.*

**LIGHTING:** Fade down.

| | |
|---|---|
| **SOUND:** | Countryside sounds. |
| **LIGHTING:** | Fade up. External.<br>A summer's day on Eston Hills. |
| **ACT II Sc IX:** | **MAUREEN is dozing, surrounded by the remnants of a picnic. Silence.<br>Children's voices get louder.<br>SUSAN appears first, followed by BILLY.** |
| **SUSAN:** | I won, Mam!! |
| **BILLY:** | Y'didn't keep to the path. |
| **SUSAN:** | I gave you a twenty second start. |

*MAUREEN is woken up.*

| | |
|---|---|
| **MAUR:** | Oh, sorry, I must I have dozed off.<br>Where's y'Dad? |
| **SUSAN:** | Here he is… a very poor third! |

*JOHN is struggling to be dignified in last place.*

| | |
|---|---|
| **MAUR:** | You alright, luv? |
| **JOHN:** | Nothing a bottle of oxygen wouldn't cure. |

*JOHN does his best to regulate his breathing.*

| | |
|---|---|
| **BILLY:** | Mam… we saw a deer being chased by a dog, but it got away. |

| | |
|---|---|
| **SUSAN:** | Came back five minutes later, checking the coast was clear. Amazing. |

*MAUREEN gets up to appreciate the view.*

| | |
|---|---|
| **SUSAN:** | And I spotted a pheasant. We almost stood on it by accident. 'Course Dad was looking at the view. |
| **MAUR:** | Wow, it's so beautiful. We should come up here more often. |
| **JOHN:** | I can't remember the last time we came up here. |
| **MAUR:** | Not since we had the kids. |

*JOHN scours the horizon.*

| | |
|---|---|
| **JOHN:** | You can see from Saltburn, all the way to Hartlepool, and that's Stockton over there. *(BILLY joins him)* None of this would be here if John Vaughan hadn't found iron. Can you imagine what it would be like? Fifteen furnaces at Eston, alone. |
| **SUSAN:** | Pretty filthy, if you ask me. |
| **JOHN:** | In 1829, only forty people lived in Middlesbrough, by 1900 there were over 90,000. That's bigger than Ayresome Park. Nearly twice as big. |
| **BILLY:** | Where'd they come from? |
| **JOHN:** | Yorkshire, Midlands, Scotland, Ireland, Wales. Don't they teach you this in school? I know I would. |

SUSAN: British Colonies, the East Indies, even from the
United States. *(She looks at JOHN)* I do listen,
Dad! *(Pause)* Oh and if you need any help
with your spelling?

BILLY: America?

JOHN: Aye. *(Jokily)* Y'know they've got nowt like
this in America!

BILLY: Really?

JOHN: Even Florida!!

*BILLY scans the skyline even more intently
and the others enjoy the moment. Silence.*

JOHN: We'll go there one day, Billy. What you
have to remember is the men and women of
Teesside iron and steel helped build famous
bridges across the world and so much more...

MAUR: And this is what we have to show for it.

*As MAUREEN joins them, they are re-united as a family.*

*Pause.*

BILLY: Can I have the last piece of cake?

JOHN: *(To BILLY)* Tidy up first?

BILLY: Why is it always me?

| | |
|---|---|
| **SUSAN:** | You always want the last mouthful. C'mon, I'll give you a hand. |
| **JOHN:** | *(To MAUREEN)* We can pop into y'Mam's if you like? |
| **MAUR:** | Yeah sure. |
| **JOHN:** | Okay, you two, we'll see you at the bottom. We'll finish this lot off. |
| **BILLY:** | We know what you'll be doing, no snoggin!! |
| **SUSAN:** | Come on... killjoy. |

*JOHN and MAUREEN watch them for a while, then turn to each other.*

| | |
|---|---|
| **SOUND:** | Vaughan Williams – The Lark Ascending floats in. |
| **JOHN:** | Let's have a toast. |
| **MAUR:** | What with? |
| **JOHN:** | The finest Champagne money can buy. |

*He mimes pouring her a glass and then one for himself.*

| | |
|---|---|
| **JOHN:** | To the future!! |
| **MAUR:** | Er okay, John... to the future! *(Pause)* I just hope the bloody kids can't see us. |

*They link arms and take another drink and enjoy the intimacy. They eventually collect their things and slowly walk of smiling.*

| | |
|---|---|
| **LIGHTING:** | Very slow fade down. |
| **SOUND:** | The music builds with a solo violin. |
| **SLIDE 36:** | *"To go along the river from Teesdale to Cleveland is like moving between two different planets. The drive from the stunning scenery to the slums of South Bank is a shaming experience. That two places should share the same country, let alone the same river… Disraeli's two nations are with us again."* The Guardian, 23rd March 1983. |
| **SLIDE 37:** | 11th June 1983. Thatcher returns with a majority of 104. |
| **SLIDE 38:** | September 1983. Ian MacGregor takes up his appointment of the National Coal Board. |
| **LIGHTING:** | Screen off. The stage is now in darkness. |
| **SOUND:** | The music fades away… |

**CURTAIN.**

# PART 3: RESOURCES

## PRODUCTION NOTES

**Venue:** Saltburn Community Theatre, Albion Terrace, Saltburn.

I originally hoped to book the Middlesbrough Theatre, but costs were quite prohibitive and we were lucky to find this venue; it had a decent stage, good dressing rooms, spaces to rehearse in and a seating capacity of 160. If we could fill them.

The play requires two main locations, Wilkinson's and the Redcar Coke Oven locker rooms, in between which has to go the screen.

So, choose your space carefully. If it is a school production, consider using the hall floor, with the audience in the round. This will give you more flexibility and the audience will get a more intimate experience.

### LIGHTING

While the play needs distinct areas/locations, an open staging is easier to accommodate a screen, what an actor friend of mine called 'pools of light', and it's easier to get any furniture on and off. It also is a lot more immediate, with characters appearing as the light goes on.

### CASTING

| Character | Details/Personality |
| --- | --- |
| Susan Wilkinson | Daughter of John and Maureen. 14 years old, a typical teenager, doesn't always do as she is told, 'fights' with her younger brother and has a mind of her own. |
| Maureen Wilkinson | Housewife and mother of Susan and Billy. Late 30s. Very supportive of husband John and loves her kids. Becomes energised by the strike. |

| | |
|---|---|
| Billy Wilkinson | 11 years old, big Boro fan and will not be pushed around by his sister. He retains his innocence, while not afraid to ask pertinent questions. |
| John Wilkinson | Hard working and well-meaning shop steward, who does his best for his work mates, who don't always appreciate his efforts. |
| Tony Simpson | Newly qualified boiler-maker, not the brightest of workers. 23 years old. A young Socialist and Tony shares his politics with anyone who will listen. |
| Mick Evans | Bit of a double-act with John. 40s. The voice of reason and a good working colleague. Mick has his own painful backstory. |
| Jeff Starforth | A lovely comic 'Jimmy Nail' type character and based on a real shop steward from Redcar Coke Oven. A joy to write. |
| Dick Graham | Former shop steward who made the move upstairs and into management, as Spares Engineer. Gamekeeper turned poacher. |
| Sheila Wallace | Salt of the earth and Maureen's best friend. Wicked humour and tells it like it is, especially to husband Brian. |
| Wendy Martin | Neighbour of Maureen and Sheila and early30s. Wants three things in life, a lovely house, a husband who goes to work every day and children. Wendy has so much to learn. |
| Brian Wallace | Boilermaker and not the brightest tool in the box. Mid 40s. Didn't strike and has his own ideas why. |
| Peter Martin | Late 30s. Process worker at ICI. Under Wendy's thumb and loves to break out, and be 'one of the lads'. When he dares to. |

## SCREEN

The slides are an essential part of the play narrative to provide a background to the strike and also give an industrial perspective. I did a presentation at Teesside University for the Landmarks: History and Heritage Conference in 2015. Afterwards, I was approached by two delegates from the Black Country, who requested if they could use my presentation as part their work on the history of the Bilston Steelworks. So, I know that it works.

## MUSIC

I don't particularly like musicals, but music is an important part of my plays, because they evoke a memory of people, time or place, and can be commentary of the time and of the action on stage. Particularly when the pieces run into the next scene and the slides.

## THE PLAYLIST

• Cavalleria Rusticana – Mascagni

• Reasons To Be Cheerful, Part 3 – Ian Dury and The Blockheads

• I Have A Dream – Abba

• Oh, Come All Ye Faithful – Traditional

• Auld Lang Syne

• Union City Blue – Blondie

• Cavatina – John Williams

• Stop the Cavalry – Jona Lewie

• Bird sounds

• The Lark Ascending – Vaughan Williams

## REMINDER

Can we remind community groups and schools that it is their responsibility to ensure their performance venues have the correct PRS Music licence, in order to use such music.

In rehearsal: The Locker Room. *(Left to right)* Stuart, Chris, Ed and Howard

Kelly reading Miller's The Crucible

Killian and Stuart. "Y'know they've got nowt like this in America."

Judith *(standing in for Sue as Maureen)* Kelly, Killian and Stuart. On Eston Hills.

Stuart just out of the shower. Has got rid of all the coke dust?

# EDUCATIONAL MATERIALS*

*"Drama demands that the students operate in an art form that uses the whole person – body, speech, intellect and spirit. I can think of no other art subject that genuinely uses all of these in its making and performance. So, drama utilises and celebrates the whole person and that includes identity in terms of culture and ethnicity."*

Drama Departments in 1992. Positive Approaches to Major Issues. Kate Bevington. Haringey Drama Adviser 1992.

The purpose of these educational materials is fourfold:

i) To have fun and explore a new published play and the many issues it raises.

ii) To put these performance activities in current examination structures across a range of units, disciplines and levels.

iii) To offer a practical focus and progression from Key Stage 4 to 5 and beyond.

iv) These practical exercises will help develop students and provide transferable knowledge and skills, whatever their career interests and choices.

*\* Written by a former GCSE and A Level Drama Examiner.*

# A WORDSEARCH FOR ALL STUDENTS: THE NATION'S FAVOURITE PLAYS 2013

In 2013, the English Touring Theatre ran a survey to find out the country's favourite plays and some 1400 plays were listed. In this exercise/activity, you have to find the top ten plays from that survey. We have given you the words in the names of the plays.

```
A Q E G J W N H N E C A A J N B I R M G
G E C I Y A I B B G V H O B L J G Z M X
Y L P S N W M Z K O M H S J F N M T P J
U M L A N S P Q S Z Y I R K I Y O F C E
H U Y H G W O V A I X S R E S K F F J R
R B A A I L R Y I J H F B I T E O I Z U
H L W M O H T S D Z T A F F Q F F M Y S
E E I F H C A I A Y F I H T E L M A H A
A R F G X I N C C I L O V B T W C X X L
R G E J N Z C X R K E I Z A R L O L F E
N Y N K J I E O A A W O F O A G R O U M
E N X Y A P K P S F T K T P N A O A Y X
S L L A C J M D Q T O C C O T K P L E B
T V O A X T J J S G E H N V H I U C D L
T P H G K I O J U P T Y Y P E X E H J E
E Y E Q P S H G S E I W T H G I N N X Z
E N G A S N D N B N L P I W V X Q O T P
N O I S E S I C B L T C H K C C X M W F
Y M A W N G A L Z Z A W C W R S O E H E
D G F C X M O M Q H I S T O R Y W B U O
```

# WORD BANK

1. Off
2. Of
3. Arcadia
4. Being
5. Inspector
6. Lear
7. Boys
8. Noises
9. The
10. Macbeth
11. Night
12. An
13. King
14. Calls
15. Earnest
16. Jerusalem
17. Twelfth
18. Hamlet
19. History
20. Importance

## WORDSEARCH: EXTENSION ACTIVITIES.

*All students:*
1. Once you have got all the play titles, can you name who wrote them?
2. Can you say which plays are in the top three? And in the right order?

*GCSE and A Level:*
3. Write a short paragraph on the top three plays saying whether you agree or disagree with their rankings.
4. Can you name the plays you would put in your top three and why?

# WJEC: GCSE in DRAMA: Sept 2022

## UNIT 1: DEVISING

All students to devise a piece of theatre in response to a stimulus. Learners must choose one stimulus from a list of four provided.

*Groups and timings*

3–4 performance students 15 minutes/20 minutes

5-6 performance students 20 minutes/30 minutes

## ASSESSMENT OF UNIT 1

1. The groups' ideas have been created and developed from the stimulus including how the techniques/characteristics of the practitioner/genre have been applied to the work.

2. The students' ideas are developed to communicate meaning through some or all of the following, in terms of form and content:

Dialogue / character / atmosphere / performance / physical and vocal skills.

All stimuli are taken from Nowt like this in America by Alan Spence.

*1. Play title:* Nowt like this in America – Alan Spence.

*2. Photograph:* Redcar Steel Complex.

3. *Song:* Reasons To Be Cheerful, Part 3 – Ian Dury and The Blockheads.
4. *Extract:*

**SLIDE 21:**          *"HUMAN BARRICADES AT THE BSC"*
                      *Angry pickets' scuffle with the police.*
                      Evening Gazette, 28th January 1980.

**LIGHTING:**          Fade Up.

**ACT I Sc IX:**       **PICKET 2.**

**PICKET 2:**          There must have been about sixty of us, all
                      screaming to be arrested. We'd been picketing
                      this Steel Depot and we formed a barrier to stop
                      lorries from bringing in supplies. Somehow,
                      the Police had managed to get between us and
                      this lorry and started chucking people out!!
                      The bloody driver took this as a signal to come
                      in and he just kept coming an' coming forward.
                      We was all pushed backwards, squashed like.
                      The next thing I knew, was a lad near me got
                      lifted up in the air and dumped, no, impaled
                      he was, on a fence. Someone said he was
                      bleeding badly and had to be taken to hospital.
                      Haven't heard how he is. *(Pause)* Then someone
                      got arrested… for obstruction so we thought,
                      fuck 'em they'll have to arrest us all.

# CHOOSE ONE PRACTITIONER.

*Katie Mitchell:*
Stanislavskian method of creating a character: the magic 'if' /
emotional memory / naturalistic movement / three dimensional
characters / use of technology to enhance the performance.

*Bertolt Brecht:*
Direct address / narrator / multi-rolling / gestus / placards / music and
songs / distancing / episodic structure / political perspectives.

*Theatre in Education:*
Target audience / topic / multi-rolling / educational information /
direct address / narrator / message / audience participation.

# AQA: GCSE DRAMA 2022.

## 1. ROLES AND RESPONSIBILITIES.
Students should develop knowledge and understanding of the roles and responsibilities of theatre makers in contemporary professional practice. Write a sentence to explain what these individual theatre makers contribute to a successful production.

playwright / performer / understudy / lighting designer / sound designer / set designer / costume designer / technician / director / stage manager / theatre manager.

**Extension:**
Chose three theatre makers and explain why you think their contributions are key to the success of a production you have seen/enjoyed. Please provide production details to support your answer.

## 2. SET PLAY: NOWT LIKE THIS IN AMERICA.
In your role as either Actor, Director or Set Designer of a future production of the play, please answer the following questions:

1. Why theatres should put on plays such as this and where it should be staged and who would be the target audience?

2. Why you would want to be involved in a new production, what you could bring to the production and what you see as the challenges?

3. Given the current socio-economic and political issues of today, what would be the pros and cons of schools studying such a play?

4. Live Performance: Digital or Streamed performance.

State the title of the live/digital theatre production you saw.

1. Describe how one or more actors used their vocal and physical skills to create one or more memorable character(s) in the production for the audience. Analyse and evaluate how successful they were in creating one or more memorable character(s) for the audience.

You could make reference to: vocal skills, for example pitch, pace and tone of voice / physical skills, for example body language and facial expression / a scene or section and/or the production as a whole.

Or

2. Describe how the set was used to communicate the themes and ideas in the production for the audience. Analyse and evaluate how successful the set was in communicating the themes and ideas in the production for the audience.

You could make reference to:

i) Materials and effects
ii) Space, scale, levels, colour
iii) A scene or section and/or the production as a whole.

# Pearson Edexcel: Level 1/ Level 2 GCSE (9-1) in Drama.

## Component 1: Devising (Component code: 1DR0/01)

All stimuli are taken from Nowt like this in America by Alan Spence.

*1. Play title:* Nowt like this in America - Alan Spence.
*2. Photograph:* Redcar Steel Complex.

*3. Song:* Reasons To Be Cheerful, Part 3 – Ian Dury and The Blockheads.
*4. Extract:*

| | |
|---|---|
| **SLIDE 21:** | *"HUMAN BARRICADES AT THE BSC"* <br> *Angry pickets' scuffle with the police.* <br> Evening Gazette, 28th January 1980. |
| **LIGHTING:** | Fade Up. |
| **ACT I Sc IX:** | **PICKET 2.** |
| **PICKET 2:** | There must have been about sixty of us, all screaming to be arrested. We'd been picketing this Steel Depot and we formed a barrier to stop |

lorries from bringing in supplies. Somehow, the Police had managed to get between us and this lorry and started chucking people out!! The bloody driver took this as a signal to come in and he just kept coming an' coming forward. We was all pushed backwards, squashed like. The next thing I knew, was a lad near me got lifted up in the air and dumped, no, impaled he was, on a fence. Someone said he was bleeding badly and had to be taken to hospital. Haven't heard how he is. *(Pause)* Then someone got arrested… for obstruction so we thought, fuck 'em they'll have to arrest us all.

# Pearson Edexcel: Level 1/ Level 2 GCSE (9-1) in Drama.

**Unit 1 overview:**
Create and develop a devised piece from a stimulus (free choice for centre).
Performance of this devised piece.
Analyse and evaluate the devising process and performance.
Assessment: AO1, AO2 and AO4. Internally assessed andexternally moderated.

**Two-part assessment:**
Portfolio covering the creating and developmental process andxanalysis and evaluation.
Submission recommendations:
Handwritten/typed evidence between 1500–2000 words.

Or

Recorded/verbal evidence between 8–10 minutes.

Or

A combination of handwritten/typed evidence (between 750–1000 words) and recorded evidence (between 4–5 minutes).

# Pearson Edexcel: Level 1
# Level 2 GCSE (9-1) in Drama.

## Unit 2 overview:

Requirements per extract: each student needs to participate in two key extracts as a performer. The timings given below are for one key extract performance.

Monologue and / or duologue students must complete a minimum monologue performance time of 2 minutes and a minimum duologue performance time of 3 minutes per extract.

The following two extracts give opportunity to act both as children, Susan and Billy who argue over money and everything else, then later in the play, their parents, John and Maureen, who have grown apart during the strike and in its aftermath.

# Nowt like this in America

| | |
|---|---|
| **ACT I Sc III:** | **BILLY and SUSAN are outside the bathroom. BILLY is counting his money. SUSAN is not impressed.** |
| **BILLY:** | 10, 11, 12… that's £13. |
| **SUSAN:** | How many more times? |
| **BILLY:** | I've had a lot of expense recently. |
| **SUSAN:** | The Boro? That's not an expense, that's a liability. |
| **BILLY:** | Who's a liar? Anyways… I don't get as much pocket money as you… 16, 18, 20… so that's £13.20. How much have you saved? |

SUSAN:          Oh, pounds!!

*She goes into the bathroom.*

BILLY:          As much as me? An' hurry up!!

SUSAN:          *(Shouts)* An' I'll have even more
                with me part-time job.

BILLY:          Part time job? Y'never out the bathroom. *(Pause)*
                I really need to go. Are y'gonna be long?

SUSAN:          Making myself even more beautiful / than ever.

BILLY:          Don't think I can wait that long. *(Beat)*

SUSAN:          *(Pops her head out)* Well y'd better start wearing
                Pampers, otherwise we won't be going to Florida!!

BILLY:          How long y' gonna be? It's not like anyone would
                wanna take you out!!

SUSAN:          You just concentrate on saving y'money and
                sorting y'plumbing out. Don't want to be going
                to Disneyland with no bedwetter, do I?

BILLY:          *(He laughs)* Well, Ian says we won't be going to
                America cos there's going to be a strike.

SUSAN:          *(Shouts)* Who?

BILLY:          His dad's a manager down Redcar Complex.
                Said no one's gonna have any money *(Beat)*
                There'll be trouble if I do a mess…

*Enter SUSAN with a towel round her head.*

**SUSAN:**        How come you know so much
               and not be potty-trained?

*SUSAN pulls a face as if she smells.*

BILLY:          Gotcha!!! *(Laughs)* Works a treat every time!!

*BILLY swans in to the bathroom. SUSAN screams as she exits.*

SUSAN:          *(Shouts)* Bet y'forgotten Christmas pressies?

BILLY:          *(Appears at the door)* Not me, all sorted.
               *(He counts again)* 1,2,3…

**SOUND:**        I Have A Dream – Abba.

**LIGHTING:**     Fade down.


**Act II Sc VII extract:**

The steel strike and John taking his redundancy have placed a massive strain on his relationship with Maureen and the children. He has to do more, but will it be enough?

*MAUREEN breathes a sigh of relief, then continues to iron her blouse. Silence.*

*JOHN enters with a bottle of sherry.*

**MAUR:**         Blimey, did they run out of beer or didn't y'win
               the Meat Draw?

**JOHN:** I said I wouldn't be late, remember?

*MAUREEN finishes the ironing and takes it out. Silence.*

**JOHN:** *(Shouting)* I've been talking to one of the lads. There's a chance of a few months' work with Davies Engineering on the complex.

*Silence. MAUREEN returns with her blouse on.*

**JOHN:** I'll go down tomorrow first thing.

**MAUR:** Those the contractors y'were calling scabs?

**JOHN:** If you can work as a cleaner, I can do that for sure.

**MAUR:** Given up on your college idea?

**JOHN:** I can do both, can't I?

*Pause.*

**MAUR:** Are you asking me or telling me?

**JOHN:** I'm.... asking you.

*MAUREEN points to the sherry.*

**MAUR:** That for me?

**JOHN:** Sherry? Since when? It's for your Mother!

**MAUR:** Sucking up to the Mafia now, are'y'?

**JOHN:** *(John gives her a look)*
She is cooking us Sunday lunch.

**MAUR:** I'm surprised y'didn't put it down
y'trousers and pretend to be The Count
of Monte Christo! *(She laughs) (Beat)*
It's never bothered you before, has it?

**JOHN:** What's that supposed to mean?

*Silence.*

**JOHN:** Well?

**MAUR:** It would appear you're appealing to me
through me Mam?

**JOHN:** Would you rather I went back to the Club?

*Silence.*

**JOHN:** I'm not a mind reader.

**MAUR:** Neither am I? Your redundancy plans, for
example?

**JOHN:** Not again, Maureen?

**MAUR:** Still don't get it, do you?

**JOHN:** I have already apologised. And I do so again.

*Silence.*

**JOHN:** I thought we were going to your Mam's?

| MAUR: | And you've bought a bottle of cheap sherry. 'Cos that's a man's job apparently. Hunter, gatherer and provider. Is that right, John? Have I missed anything? |
| --- | --- |
| JOHN: | She is expecting us. |
| MAUR: | And all I had to do was cook, sew and clean for you and the kids. Remember them? |

*Silence. MAUREEN goes out and returns with her coat, and puts it on.*

| JOHN: | Maureen, I know you don't believe me. |
| --- | --- |
| MAUR: | Let me finish, John! You see when I took the cleaning job, I wasn't attacking you, John, I was trying to feed my family, that's all it was. That's all it ever was. Looking after my family. Right? Just like you. |

*Silence.*

| JOHN: | I realise now, I shouldn't have taken it out on… you and the kids. |
| --- | --- |
| MAUR: | God, you were just so… angry… all the time. I've never seen you… |
| JOHN: | I know, I brought it all home. Every bit of it. |

*JOHN stands like a little boy lost…*

| JOHN: | So, is that it then? |
| --- | --- |

*Silence.*

**MAUR:** Think… I'm gonna kick you out?

*Silence.*

**MAUR:** Oh, I'm not letting you off the hook that easily.

**JOHN:** Woo!! What'y'talkin about?

**MAUR:** Listen to me now. You get some contract work, till college starts. It'll keep you out of my way, if nothing else.

*Pause.*

**MAUR:** Thinking of getting a proper office job, rather than just cleaning it.

**JOHN:** With 21 hours study a week, I can still claim. A Tory councillor told me.

**MAUR:** And you believed him?
Well, you're gonna have to trust me.

**JOHN:** Trust you? What you talking about?
Is that a yes, then?

**MAUR:** Did you tell them about your spelling?

**JOHN:** won't, if you won't? *(Beat)*
Are we going to your mother's?

*Silence.*

**JOHN:** It would be a shame to waste a cheap bottle of British sherry.

**MAUR:**          If you weren't so much like...

*They stare at each other for a while and JOHN tentatively opens his arms for a hug. Silence. MAUREEN returns the embrace. They get their things and exit.*

**LIGHTING:**     Fade down.

# PEARSON BTEC Level 3 National: Extended Diploma in Performing Arts Practice.

## MODULE H: COLLABORATIVE PERFORMING ARTS PROJECT

### ASSESSMENT OBJECTIVES:

H20: Plan and prepare for a creative or administrative role, clear demonstration of your skills in your chosen role and contribute to the successful completion of your group project.

H21: Demonstrate personal engagement and responsibility when developing a collaborative project. Incorporate your performance skills to enhance the project development, and continuous collaboration to achieve a successful outcome.

H22: Demonstrate technical and interpretive performance skills in a collaborative project leading to a successful project.

Your chosen project should be based around the many opportunities possible through the study of Nowt like this in America.

### 1. A SHORT PLAY/SELECTED SCENES:

A selection of scenes to explore the issues in the play to help develop audience understanding, Engage the workshop in a range of activities to deepen the experience and understanding of the play's characters, situations and background.

*Activities could include:* warm up games and exercises, hot seating, acting out scenes, explore whether the characters had choices, alternative things they could have done?

Peer group feedback and q & a to discern what the groups have understood and learnt.

Possible feedback form to ascertain a wider experience of the participants and sessions should photographed to provide evidence for student assessment.

## PRACTITIONERS:

*Brecht:* Direct address / narrator / multi-rolling / gestus / placards / music and songs / distancing / episodic structure / political perspectives.

*Augusto Boal:* Promoting social political change / Interactive Theatre / forum Theatre / image Theatre / short scenes with a strong image that the audience can easily understand and identify with.

## 2. A COMMUNITY PROJECT:

Using the play to reflect on real people's lives and local historical events to create a series of group presentations. Starting with a short presentation of key facts, characters and actions. Using the theme music from the play: ask the participants what the music suggests to them? Who are the characters in the narrative, where are these people? What is happening in their story.

*Activity:* In small groups, the actors have to create an opening sequence of no more than thirty seconds. Time to prepare and the share with the class.

Peer group feedback and q & a to discern what the groups have understood and learnt.

Activity: To follow up, each group is given a card with a track from the play on and they have to create a short scene where the music is played at the end. Time to prepare and then share with the class.

Peer group feedback and q & a to discern what the groups have understood and learnt.

Possible feedback form to ascertain a wider experience of the participants and sessions should photographed to provide evidence for student assessment.

## PRACTITIONERS:

*Marianne Elliott:* Using all aspects of theatre making /
physical theatre / songs / music / Brechtian techniques.

*Berkoff:* Stylised movement (slow motion / robotic)
exaggerated facial expressions / direct address / tableaux /
ensemble playing / Minimalism.

*In your projects, you should explore and develop
collaborative performance skills, to include:*

i) Consider your target audience, their interests and needs.
Why would this project appeal to them?

ii) Discussing and sharing creative ideas.

iii) Using stimuli, such as style, practitioners, and existing material
from the play.

iv) How will you engage and encourage participation in your
workshops and exploration?

v) Developing, refining and presenting your material.

Students will be expected to explore and try at least two different roles
or responsibilities, essential for successful completion of their project:

Artistic director / budget manager / designer / event manager /
promoter / social media manager / technical manager / liaison

*To gain understanding and experience in planning, students should explore the following organisational skills in their roles:*

i)creating and working to schedules

ii)budgeting

ii) sourcing resources and equipment

iii) developing a promotional strategy

iv) developing and designing materials and marketing ideas

vi) addressing legal considerations; risk assessment, health and safety.

# Pearson Edexcel:
# A Level Drama and Theatre. (9DR0).

**1. Devising:** An original performance piece, using one key extract from a performance text and a theatre practitioner as stimuli.

*Group size:* 3–4 performance students 15 mins to 20 mins.
5-6 performance students 20 mins to 30 mins.

Devising skills should include the following:

i) The deconstruction of ideas, themes and narratives that make up the stimuli.

ii) Using appropriate methods that interpret the stimuli, being able to reposition it and see it differently.

iii) Carry out in-depth research to inform and develop ideas and creativity.

iv) Give and respond to ideas in a group context.

v) Develop their exploratory skills through: workshops / rehearsal / taught classes / individual research / watching live theatre.

## Nowt like this in America by Alan Spence.

The following extract offers two scenes: one in the Wilkinson family home and the other at John Wilkinson's place of work. In addition, intertitles add historical, socio-economic and political background.

Themes to explore: Family life, relationships, sibling rivalry, hopes and dreams, gender stereotypes, working in heavy industry, management-worker tensions, cost of living issues, political interference in the workplace, perceptions of an industry.

## PRACTITIONERS: CHOOSE ONE.

*Joan Littlewood:* Agitprop Theatre: For actors, this meant becoming a voice for opposing arguments and points of view, rather than changing their audience through catharsis, actors would appeal, persuade and antagonise their audiences.

*Popular Theatre:* Joan employed acting styles from Commedia Dell'arte, which uses stock characters, and slapstick to engage audiences and undermine theatrical tradition.

*Creative Ensemble:* Included not just acting but everything else from administration to making sets and costumes. This approach developed a trust and understanding between the company that freed up creative possibility and led to productions outside of the theatrical norm.

*Steven Berkoff:* Focuses on the physical abilities of the performers as a substitute for sets and props, often known as total theatre Berkoff's work is influenced by Ancient Greek theatre, Japanese Noh and Kabuki, Shakespeare, East End music halls and his Jewish heritage Berkoff also uses the techniques of practitioners such as Artaud and Brecht in his work.

# ACT I. SC 1:

**SLIDE 1:**    Nowt like this in America by Alan Spence

**SLIDE 2:**    *"Trade union power in the UK interferes with market forces, causing inflation, and has to be checked, to restore the 'profitability' of the UK. I and others also believe it necessary to check union power in the aftermath of the fall of the Heath government, in the face of the 1974 strikes."* Nicholas Ridley MP, The Ridley Report, 1977.

**SOUND:**    Cavalleria Rusticana music floats in the background.

**SLIDE 3:**    In 1850, John Vaughan discovers ironstone at Eston.

In 1851, the first blast furnace is blown in.

By 1861, over forty furnaces on Teesside.

**SLIDE 4:**    *"This remarkable place, the youngest child of England's enterprise, is an infant, but if an infant, an infant Hercules."*
W.E. Gladstone, Middlesbrough, 1862.

**SLIDE 5:**    *"The story, the marvellous story, of its rise. The idea symbolised by its history, is force – a physical, mental and moral force."*

**SLIDE 6:**    *"Which enables communities to wrestle with, and overcome obstacles, which circumstances cast in their way. As they struggle upwards and onwards, to a better state of living."*
Joseph Cowans, Middlesbrough Jubilee, 1881.

**SLIDE 7:**    August 1979.

**LIGHTING:**    Fade up. Interior. The Wilkinson's.
Late afternoon.

**ACT 1 SC1:**    The music continues to build and we see SUSAN WILKINSON, aged 15 moving / conducting the music, in a world of her own. A woman appears, MAUREEN WILKINSON, aged 36, her Mam.

*MAUREEN puts down her bags and enters.*

MAUR:                  Susan, Susan!! Don't you know your father's
                       in bed?

*MAUREEN goes and turns the music down.*

SUSAN:                 Sorry. / Didn't see you there.

MAUR:                  Shift relief. Nights tonight, and tomorrow.

SUSAN:                 On his birthday?

MAUR:                  Can't always choose y'days off. Seen our Billy?

SUSAN:                 Yes, but he went straight out again.

MAUR:                  If he's playing football again, I'll hit him so hard
                       he won't know whether it's  Shrove Tuesday
                       or Sheffield Wednesday. *(She notices the table)*
                       Thanks for setting the table, luv.
                       Look what I've got for y'Dad.

*She exits and returns with a cake.*

MAUR:                  What d'y'think?

SUSAN:                 One candle?

MAUR:                  He'd be upset if we didn't get him a cake, even
                       more, if we put the right number of candles on.

*They both laugh.*

SUSAN:                 I got a card and signed it of course... just in case.

**MAUR:**     If he doesn't show soon, he's for the high jump.

*They put the card at John's place.*

*Enter BILLY WILKINSON, aged 11, with a card in his hand.*

**BILLY:**     Hi Mam!

**MAUR:**     Shh!! *(whispering)* Where the hell have you been?

**BILLY:**     Been to get me Dad a card.

*MAUREEN and SUSAN are gob-smacked.*

**MAUR:**     Right. Well go and wash now and don't wake your dad. *(BILLY Exits)* Y'know, if he wasn't so much like his Dad, he wouldn't last five minutes round here.

*Enter JOHN WILKINSON half awake.*

**JOHN:**     Mam! You shouldn't have bothered…

**MAUR:**     Sorry love, I was going to give you another fifteen minutes.

*MAUREEN kisses his cheek.*

**JOHN:**     I was being serenaded, wasn't I, Susan?

**SUSAN:**     Sorry, Dad.

*SUSAN offers a chair to JOHN. He sits down.*

| | |
|---|---|
| **MAUR:** | Susan, make some tea, luv; the kettle should've boiled. |

*SUSAN goes and BILLY returns.*

| | |
|---|---|
| **BILLY:** | Happy birthday Dad!! |
| **JOHN:** | Hello son… thank you. |
| **BILLY:** | Have you seen me card yet, Dad? |
| **MAUR:** | When we're all at the table… Did you wash? |
| **BILLY:** | Yes. *(He offers his hands)* |

*SUSAN brings in tea and puts it on the table.*

| | |
|---|---|
| **BILLY:** | Can I have some Coke? |
| **JOHN:** | Please? |
| **BILLY:** | Please! |

*BILLY pours himself a drink, leaving the bottle on the table.*
*JOHN looks and he puts the bottle on the floor.*

| | |
|---|---|
| **JOHN:** | Who's going to say grace? |

*There is a short pause.*

| | |
|---|---|
| **ALL:** | Grace!! |

*They all laugh.*

| | |
|---|---|
| **JOHN:** | And Billy, it's not a race. |

*He opens BILLY's card; it has footballers on. He reads it.*

**JOHN:**          Thanks, Billy. Want to go to see the Boro
                   on Saturday?

**BILLY:**         Can we, Dad? Please?

**JOHN:**          We'll see.

*He opens SUSAN's card; it's got boats on.*

**JOHN:**          Oh, thanks luv.

*She kisses him and gives him the album, as his present.*
*The one she has been playing.*

**JOHN:**          What have I done to deserve this? *(He reads)*
                   Beethoven, Elgar and Mascagni, so that's what
                   I was listening to?

**SUSAN:**         Sorry, Dad…

**BILLY:**         I wanted to buy you Abba.

**SUSAN:**         Y'supposed to buy them something they like.

**BILLY:**         You chose it, not me.

**JOHN:**          That's enough, Billy. It's a lovely surprise, Susan,
                   thank you both.

*He reads MAUREEN's card and they exchange smiles.*

**BILLY:**         How many kisses, Dad?

| | |
|---|---|
| **SUSAN:** | Don't be rude! |
| **BILLY:** | *(Whispers)* You didn't even wrap it up! |
| **MAUR:** | Haven't got you anything yet, luv. |
| **JOHN:** | I know, it's difficult. The man who has everything. |

*JOHN puts his hand out and touches MAUREEN's.*

| | |
|---|---|
| **MAUR:** | There are still one or two sales on, we might pick up a bargain on Saturday. |
| **JOHN:** | Just remember, pet… no socks please, we're British! |

*BILLY doesn't get the joke and SUSAN groans.*

| | |
|---|---|
| **SUSAN:** | Dad? |

*Silence. BILLY is nodding his head for all he is worth, to get SUSAN to speak up.*

| | |
|---|---|
| **SUSAN:** | Dad-dy… |
| **BILLY:** | What she is trying to say is are we going to America or what? |
| **SUSAN:** | Can you just shut!! |
| **JOHN:** | Can you two stop squabbling? (He puts his knife down and thinks) Well, Mam and I have thought about it carefully and at length. |

**BILLY:** We're not gonna go, are we?

**SUSAN:** Shush, will y'?

**JOHN:** *(He continues)* The cost of everything, what we can afford, what we can save… or just go to Benidorm again?

**SUSAN:** Oh please? You promised…

**JOHN:** It is… an awful lot of money.

**BILLY:** I told you, didn't I?

**JOHN:** So, we'd better put down a deposit on Saturday!!

*BILLY and SUSAN didn't believe what they heard, don't react and then uproar.*

**SUSAN:** And can we go to Disneyland?

**BILLY:** And the NASA Space Station!!

**JOHN:** You'll have to pull your weight and help around the house or we won't be going anywhere!

*SUSAN and BILLY are full of promises, much to JOHN and Maureen's amusement.*

**SOUND:** Reasons To Be Cheerful, Part 3 – Ian Dury and The Blockheads

**LIGHTING:** Fade down.

| | |
|---|---|
| **SLIDE 8:** | The Ridley Report on Nationalised Industries 1977. |
| | Regulate wages and buy off powerful groups. |
| | State powers used to break strikes. |
| | A large mobile police force to stop picketing. |
| | Vulnerable groups identified as Railway, Civil Service and the Steel Industry. |
| | The report only came to light when leaked to The Economist in 1978. |
| | |
| **LIGHTING:** | Fade up. Coke Ovens. Locker room. Early morning. |
| | |
| **SOUND:** | Fade off music. |
| | |
| **ACT I Sc II:** | **Coke Ovens. Locker room.** |
| | **JEFF STANFORTH 30s, a labourer, is reading The Sun.** |
| | **MICK EVANS 40s, electrician, drinks tea.** |
| | |
| **JEFF:** | Eh! Listen to this… "Dear Claire Rayner, my father died nearly eighteen months ago, and I now have bouts of depression, even tears. I am nineteen and male, is there anything wrong with me?" What is the bloody country coming to? |

*Silence.*

| | |
|---|---|
| **MICK:** | When my father died… about three weeks afterwards, I just broke down and cried, I couldn't stop. Couldn't stop for ten to fifteen minutes. It was only then that I realised; he would never beat me again. |
| | |
| **JEFF:** | Bloody hell, Mick… Y'never said… |

| MICK: | I took our Andrew back to Catterick, and just before we left, he gave me a big hug. I couldn't handle it. Why? I love him. *(Pause)* What does Auntie Clare say then? |
|---|---|
| JEFF: | Oh, it's all normal and he must have had a good relationship with his father. We're breeding a load of bloody poofters, if you ask me. |
| V.O: | Gaffers coming. |
| JEFF: | Fucking hell!! *(He makes a quick exit)* |

*Enter TONY SIMPSON mid 20s, boilermaker, with a BSC Breakfast.*

| TONY: | Works every time… |
| MICK: | Still playing Russian Roulette with the canteen then? |
| TONY: | Best meal of the day, man. |

*JEFF returns.*

| TONY: | Got y'quicker than a Hartlepool Cod, Jeff. You losing it? |
| JEFF: | Y'don't get five minutes peace in here, as it is. |
| TONY: | You wouldn't be much use in the Revolution, comrade. |
| JEFF: | An' don't comrade me. Y'have as much chance of getting a revolution in this country, as Scargill getting a Knighthood. |

| MICK: | Let's face it, Labour MPs are a more endangered species than the blue whale. |
|---|---|

*Enter JOHN covered in coke dust.*

| JEFF: | Even shop stewards aren't safe these days, eh John? |
|---|---|
| TONY: | Where y' working? |
| JOHN: | Dolls House. Fifth floor. Give us a hand, will y'? |
| TONY: | Er... I'd love to, but... |
| JOHN: | I know... job requires a tradesman and you're a boilermaker. |
| JEFF: | Only on his mother's side though. |
| MICK: | Cards at dinner time, John? |
| JOHN: | Sorry, got a Health and Safety meeting at 12.30. |
| MICK: | Hope y'goin to tell them we'd like some? |
| JOHN: | Exactly! Do us a favour, Mick, and finish it for us, would'ya? I'm sure I got it to keep me out of the meeting. |
| MICK: | Much to do? |
| JOHN: | Cables to connect, it's all in place, tools on the job. |

| | |
|---|---|
| **JEFF:** | Bit risky John, you don't know what you might lose? |
| **TONY:** | Why? You working up there? |
| **MICK:** | Yeah, alright John, but don't forget you owe me one? |
| **JOHN:** | Cheers, Mick. Hope I can get this shite off and be human again. |

*He exits.*

| | |
|---|---|
| **JEFF:** | John, what did you mean? Why are you working up there? |
| **TONY:** | Don't ask me… Fagin. |

*TONY flicks food at JEFF and escapes. JEFF responds.*

| | |
|---|---|
| **JEFF:** | I'll fucking Fagin y', y' cheeky bastard. |
| **MICK:** | Children please. |
| **V.O:** | There's people trying to get to sleep, in here. |
| **SOUND:** | Money – Pink Floyd. |
| **LIGHTING:** | Fade down. |

# 2. Theatre in Performance: A Duologue.

*Content:* A group performance realisation of one key extract from a performance text. A monologue or duologue performance from one key extract from a different performance text.

*Assessment:* AO2 is assessed. Externally assessed either by visiting examiner or by examiner assessing the recorded live performance.

*Performance time:* Duologue 5 – 6 minutes.

*Requirements for performances:* All performances should take place in front of an appropriate audience and must be recorded. Centres are free to identify their own suitable audience and venue for the performance, this could include: performance to the rest of the class or another class within the centre. A performance to an invited external audience.


Nowt like this in America by Alan Spence

*The following extract is taken from Act II Scene VII, where John and Maureen have fallen out big time and John has to mend the bridges. He's failing badly.*

**MAUR:**  Blimey, did they run out of beer or didn't y'win the Meat Draw?

**JOHN:**  I said I wouldn't be late, remember?

*MAUREEN finishes the ironing and takes it out. Silence.*

**JOHN:**  (*Shouting*) I've been talking to one of the lads. There's a chance of a few months' work with Davies Engineering on the complex.

*Silence. MAUREEN returns with her blouse on.*

| | |
|---|---|
| **JOHN:** | I'll go down tomorrow first thing. |
| **MAUR:** | Those the contractors y'were calling scabs? |
| **JOHN:** | If you can work as a cleaner, I can do that for sure. |
| **MAUR:** | Given up on your college idea? |
| **JOHN:** | I can do both, can't I? |

*Pause.*

| | |
|---|---|
| **MAUR:** | Are you asking me or telling me? |
| **JOHN:** | I'm…. asking you. |

*MAUREEN points to the sherry.*

| | |
|---|---|
| **MAUR:** | That for me? |
| **JOHN:** | Sherry? Since when? It's for your Mother! |
| **MAUR:** | Sucking up to the Mafia now, are'y'? |
| **JOHN:** | *(John gives her a look)* She is cooking us Sunday lunch. |
| **MAUR:** | I'm surprised y'didn't put it down y'trousers and pretend to be The Count of Monte Christo! *(She laughs) (Beat)* It's never bothered you before, has it? |
| **JOHN:** | What's that supposed to mean? |

*Silence.*

**JOHN:**  Well?

**MAUR:**  It would appear, you're appealing to me,
through me Mam?

**JOHN:**  Would you rather I went back to the Club?

*Silence.*

**JOHN:**  I'm not a mind reader.

**MAUR:**  Neither am I? Your redundancy plans,
for example?

**JOHN:**  Not again, Maureen?

**MAUR:**  Still don't get it, do you?

**JOHN:**  I have already apologised. And I do so again.

*Silence.*

**JOHN:**  I thought we were going to your Mam's?

**MAUR:**  And you've bought a bottle of cheap sherry.
'Cos that's a man's job apparently. Hunter,
gatherer and provider. Is that right, John?
Have I missed anything?

**JOHN:**  She is expecting us.

**MAUR:**  And all I had to do was cook, sew and clean for
you and the kids. Remember them?

*Silence. MAUREEN goes out and returns with her coat, and puts it on.*

**JOHN:**          Maureen, I know you don't believe me.

**MAUR:**        Let me finish, John! You see when I took the
cleaning job, I wasn't attacking you, John,
I was trying to feed my family, that's all it was.
That's all it ever was. Looking after my family.
Right? Just like you.

*Silence.*

**JOHN:**          I realise now, I shouldn't have taken it out on…
you and the kids.

**MAUR:**        God, you were just so… angry… all the time.
I've never seen you…

**JOHN:**          I know, I brought it all home. Every bit of it.

*JOHN stands like a little boy lost…*

**JOHN:**          So, is that it then?

*Silence.*

**MAUR:**        Think… I'm gonna kick you out?

*Silence.*

**MAUR:**        Oh, I'm not letting you off the hook that easily.

**JOHN:**          Woo!! What'y'talkin about?

| | |
|---|---|
| **MAUR:** | Listen to me now. You get some contract work, till college starts. It'll keep you out of my way, if nothing else. |

*Pause.*

| | |
|---|---|
| **MAUR:** | Thinking of getting a proper office job, rather than just cleaning it. |
| **JOHN:** | With 21 hours study a week, I can still claim. A Tory councillor told me. |
| **MAUR:** | And you believed him? Well, you're gonna have to trust me. |
| **JOHN:** | Trust you? What you talking about? Is that a yes then? |
| **MAUR:** | Did you tell them about your spelling? |
| **JOHN:** | I won't, if you won't? *(Beat)* Are we going to your Mother's? |

*Silence.*

| | |
|---|---|
| **JOHN:** | It would be a shame to waste a cheap bottle of British sherry. |
| **MAUR:** | If you weren't so much like… |

*They stare at each other for a while and JOHN tentatively opens his arms for a hug. Silence. MAUREEN returns the embrace. They get their things and exit.*

| | |
|---|---|
| **LIGHTING:** | Fade down. |

# GETTING THE PLAY ON THE STAGE*

What does it take to be a playwright in the community? My reflections on the highs and lows of writing plays for community groups over the last 25 years featured recently on the arts professional web site.

Made redundant from British Steel in 1980, my passion for drama and theatre took me back to college to do teacher training. I spent many happy years as a drama practitioner in schools and in 2009 decided to form my own company, Theatre is Real Life.

Four plays, three productions, many rejections and one education pack later, it is time for reflection.

My first play, 'Two Sisters' back in 1990, was the product of a playwriting workshop at the Holborn Centre for Performing Arts in London. Based on a true event about some legal documents that were found in the street, it explores older people's attitudes and relationships. The workshop ended with rehearsed readings by professional actors.

My second play 'Nowt like this in America', set around the 1980 steel strike, is the story of a family, a community and an industry. I submitted the play to Alasdair Ramsey of Cleveland Theatre Company, who liked it and advised me, and it would be one of five new plays to receive a rehearsed reading as part of a New Writing North programme at Live Theatre in Newcastle over five nights.

This was a minimal performance in that two days of rehearsal gave the actors a working knowledge of the script. Would a full production follow? As I am London-based and the production was to be in the North East of England, I attempted to draw funding from Newcastle and London.

After several frustrating months arguing with funders about issues such as heritage, 'Nowt' only went ahead courtesy of a pension pot, my very understanding family and my undying enthusiasm (others might say vanity).

My third play was inspired by Peter Terson's football play 'Zigger Zagger' on teenage football fans and their rites of passage into the adult world of work. We relocated our production from Stoke to Middlesbrough, and when Middlesbrough Football Club nearly went out of business in 1986, then won its first trophy in 2004, the desire to put that story on stage loomed large.

Workshops in local schools nearly happened, but a combination of costs and other commitments meant we drew a blank. Four months later, I had written the play, 'The BORO's 37mins'.

Staging the production at Middlesbrough College only a corner kick from the Middlesbrough FC Riverside Stadium, seemed fortuitous. But good coverage in the local media could not overcome some of the problems, people not knowing where the college was, just one of the issues. The small audience that did see the play were not disappointed and a critical rather than commercial success provided some comfort.

2011 was the twenty-fifth anniversary of Middlesbrough FC coming back from the brink and temptation reared its head again. Mindful of the heritage issue and funding, I discovered the way forwards: education activities could link with heritage, while giving opportunities to arts practitioners, football fans and the wider community.

As a member of the Independent Theatre Council, I aided my professional development through a series workshops, and a key thread that emerged was that you can't do things on your own.

To this end, I engaged an arts consultancy and Middlesbrough 86 was born. The two consultants were crucial in securing Heritage Lottery funding and some £120,000 in support in kind, while I was able to secure the support of Mark White of the Vice Principal's office Teesside University, which provided a promotional film, rehearsal space and theatre, a DVD of the production and launched the education pack.

More recently, I read an article about teenage relationships and sexting, and I decided to write a play about how teenage relationships had moved on to a dangerous new level. With funding from Awards for All, and workshops with Ghetto Youth Theatre (GYT) under the guidance of Face Front Inclusive Theatre, where I am a trustee, I developed my fourth play about cyber-bullying, sexting, revenge porn and grooming with a working title 'Cybermissive'.

GYT decided not to use the script and at the 11th hour, I redrafted and renamed it 'My name is Tom'. The rejections continued so I edited the play to suit schools' needs and offered a range of free activities. Four schools have joined the education project and I was very pleased that a production of My Name is Tom was performed at the Dugdale Centre Theatre in Enfield, North London in January 2016.

With this experience and the experience I have gained since writing this article, I hope you will find these thoughts useful if you too want to be a playwright, community or otherwise.

• *Writing:* You need to write every day. Anything will do, just get into the writing habit. Once you have established a regular writing schedule, decide what is best for you, how long you can write for. Try this for a month and then reflect… do you need to up the amount of time you write or can you reduce your daily input? You should stay in control of the process. The other thing about getting started, once you put words on the page, your memory and imagination can go into overdrive.

• *Timing:* Another issue is that when things are going well, you suddenly find you have been writing/working for three/four or five hours without a break. That is not good, you should build in comfort breaks, so you don't get tired or stressed out.

• *Other commitments:* As a writer you are on your own, but you have work, family, friends and hobbies, all that will need to be addressed. So you must ensure your writing time becomes sacrosanct, but not at the expense of your work, family hobbies and well-being. When things are tough you need to be able to handle all the aspects of writing, which includes your other responsibilities. know why you are doing it and if there is a need for what you are offering. Check what others are doing and what is happening in your area, so you don't miss out.

• *Reading other playwrights:* Can't stress this enough, we can learn so much from other writers, because they can teach us, spark our imaginations, take us to different places, times and themes. If you're not enjoying one, put it down and read another. Even better go to the theatre. Youth, community or professional/commercial... all can offer a learning experience.

• *Structures:* In the first instance, make a list of possible characters and decide who is the main person, your protagonist. Every scene has to really be about them. Unless of course it's a thematic issue within a community, a strike, a tragic event, a celebration, the history of a community or building, area.

I sometimes use a table 3 acts to 5 acts columns wide, with the acts numbered across the top and the scenes numbered down the side. The purpose of this is to mechanically plot your play, so you have a visual record of your ideas. Then you can move them around, take them out, rewrite your ideas. It helps you realise where you have been and where you want to go.

• *What to write:* Yes, write from experience, which is what I have done with my first two plays, but the next three are beyond my experience, inspired by stories, events and community issues.

Simon Stephens, writer of so many plays draws on his experience using photographs, all kinds of music, other books, paintings. Inspiration can come from anywhere.

• *Research:* You may think this is time consuming, but this is a valid activity for a variety of reasons: i) It could provide relevant and new information/detail you weren't aware of. ii) Research helps to base your work in reality, in real places, characters and issues – regardless of the genre of writing you are doing. iii) It can also fire the imagination to offer new characters, action and dialogue that you won't believe.

• *What to do when you have finished:* Firstly, well done. Invite family and friends round to do a reading. They can use various electronic devices, so cutting down on printing. Listen to what they have to say, there may be sound advice for us, suggestions to develop and improve what you have written.

If your work is ready for a more discerning and critical eye, share it with youth, community and amateur companies. You can also submit plays to competitions in your local area. Also theatres do have periods where they welcome plays from unproduced/unpublished writers.

There are also two key competitions for new writers. The Papatango and the Bruntwood Prize.

• *Planning:* Youth, community and amateur companies often programme 12 to 18 months in advance so you need to be aware of that when making an approach.

• *Schools:* Why not offer free activities to schools in your area, where you may have links through your children, family and friends, such as assemblies, discussion groups and workshops. Remember you would need to have a DBS certificate to work with schools.

• *Funding:* There is advice online, through the Arts Council, which is the leading funder. But also ask friends or people in local arts communities who may have applied and/or received funding if they can advise you.

• *Networks:* Link with other developing playwrights in your area and don't be afraid to ask professionals for advice. Look for free opportunities or cheap events, including websites for community organisations, to promote your work. Social networks are helpful in this regard, such as Twitter and Facebook.

• *Marketing:* Business cards and leaflets are always useful to build links and promote what you do. If you don't think you have something to offer, why should anyone else?

Social media is also a great way to get your work out there and generate interest in what you are doing. I have recently gone from a WordPress website to a blog and find it so much easier to write and manage.

• *Insurance:* Join a writing organisation that includes public liability cover as part of its membership fee, such as National Association of Writers in Education. There is also the Writers' Guild of Great Britain, covering everything from books, plays, films, radio, comics, computer games and podcasts. Other groups include: the Society of Authors, The National Association of Writers' Groups, and Writers' Services, all offering a range of guidance and help.

• *Self-publishing:* This is a growing industry and now recognised by many organisations and individuals as a very good way into getting your work into the public domain. There are many writers who have publishing deals and agents, who still choose to self-publish on occasion to have complete control of the writing and output.

There are any number of publishing outlets, but I have chosen Amazon and their Kindle Direct Publishing. Why? Because it is one of the best and provide a good quality service. But that is your choice to make.

I would also like to mention Sixth Element Publishing based in Billingham, who had never published a play before and this is their second. They are excellent, and on your doorstep in Teesside, but they also work with people across the UK and the wider world in many countries. Well worth considering.

Alan Spence is a community playwright and was Artistic Director of Theatre is Real Life Productions till 2018.

*This article first appeared in Arts Professional in Dec 2014, many things have changed, not least with Brexit, Covid and the funding in the Arts generally and I have updated the information accordingly.

** The play script and handbook will be published in the autumn 2024.

# SOURCES OF MATERIAL

Page 27. Richard III / Comedy of Errors. Shakespeare in Performance. Consultant Editors Keith Parsons & Pamela Mason. Salamander 1995.

Page 32. Angels in America. PLAYED IN BRITAIN: MODERN THEATRE IN 100 PLAYS. Kate Dorney & Frances Gray. metheun I drama 2013.

Page 46. Black Watch. PLAYED IN BRITAIN: MODERN THEATRE IN 100 PLAYS. Kate Dorney & Frances Gray. metheun I drama 2013.

Page 49. Mark Lawson. Alan Bennett's play The Madness of George III has new relevance in 2018. *www.newstatesman.com/culture/theatre/2018/11/the-madness-of-george-iii-alan-bennett-nottingham-playhouse-brexit*

# NEW WRITING PLAY COMPETITIONS

**Papatango New Writing Prize**
Usually opens in February.
Offering anonymous assessment of plays.
*www.papatango.co.uk/new-writing-prize/*

**The Bruntwood Prize - Approximate dates**
January: Open for submissions
June: Submission close
June: Phase One Reading Complete
July: Phase Two Reading Complete
August: Phase 3 Reading Complete
September: Longlist of Top 100 Plays Announced
October: Shortlist Announced
November: Bruntwood Prize for Playwriting Ceremony
December: Deadline for Feedback sent to Longlist Plays
*www.writeaplay.co.uk*

## Examination Board links

AQA GCSE Drama
*www.aqa.org.uk/subjects/drama/gcse/drama-8261*

AQA Advanced Level Drama and Theatre
*www.aqa.org.uk/subjects/drama/a-level/drama-and-theatre-7262*

BTEC in Performing Arts | Pearson qualifications
*www.qualifications.pearson.com/en/subjects/
drama-theatre-studies-and-performing-arts/btec-performing-arts.html*

GCSE Drama (2016) | Pearson qualifications
*www.qualifications.pearson.com/en/qualifications/edexcel-gcses/
drama-2016.html*

A level Drama and Theatre (2016) | Pearson qualifications
*www.qualifications.pearson.com/en/qualifications/edexcel-a-levels/
drama-and-theatre-2016.html*

Welsh Joint Education Committee GCSE Drama - *www.wjec.co.uk*

## Other writing links

Writers' Guild of Great Britain - *www.writersguild.org.uk*

National Association of Writers in Education - *www.nawe.co.uk*

The Society of Authors - *www.thesocietyofauthors.org*

National Association of Writers' Groups - *www.nawg.co.uk*

Writers' Services - *www.writersservices.com*

# Afterword

*For more information, please go to:*
**nowmeetthewriteralanspence.blogspot.com**